John Hughes

telephone
English

Includes phrase bank, audio CD and role plays

Macmillan Education
4 Crinan Street
London N1 9XW
A division of Springer Nature Limited
Companies and representatives throughout the world

ISBN-13: 978-1-4050-8219-8
ISBN-10: 1-4050-8219-4

Text © John Hughes 2006
Design and illustration © Springer Nature Limited 2006

First published 2006

All rights reserved; no part of this publication may be reproduced, stored in a retrieval system, transmitted in any form, or by any means, electronic, mechanical, photocopying, recording, or otherwise, without the prior written permission of the publishers.

Original design by Mike Brain Graphic Design Limited, Oxford
Page make-up by Keith Shaw, Threefold Design Ltd
Illustrated by Willie Ryan
Cover design by Andrew Oliver
Cover photograph by Corbis

The authors and publishers would like to thank the following photographers and artists for permission to reproduce their photographic material:
CartoonStock/www.CartoonStock.com pp6, 16, 21 and 28; Nishant Choksi p36; Getty Images/Javier Pierini p40, Getty Images/Stephen Shepherd p52; Reuters/Sherwin Crasto p54.

The author would like to thank Karen Spiller and to dedicate the book to Jerzy Nanowski.

Whilst every effort has been made to locate the owners of copyright material in this book, there may have been some cases when the publishers have been unable to contact the owners. We should be grateful to hear from anyone who recognises copyright material and who is unacknowledged. We shall be pleased to make the necessary amendments in future editions of the book.

Printed and bound in Great Britain by Ashford Colour Press Ltd.

2019
20 19

Contents

To the student		4
To the teacher		5
Essentials	1 Answering the phone	6
	2 Making and taking calls	8
	3 Reasons for calling	10
	4 Leaving messages	12
	5 Taking messages	14
	6 Asking the caller to wait	16
	7 Asking for repetition and clarifying	18
	8 Ending the call	20
	9 Language review 1	22
Everyday phone calls	10 Booking hotels and restaurants	24
	11 Booking transport	26
	12 Dealing with telephone problems	28
	13 Recorded information and phone menus	30
	14 Leaving voicemail messages	32
	15 Language review 2	34
Telephone skills	16 Sounding friendly and polite	36
	17 Planning a call	38
	18 Telephone manner	40
	19 Small talk	42
	20 Formal and informal	44
	21 Language review 3	46
Phone calls with customers/colleagues	22 Making appointments	48
	23 Inviting people	50
	24 Confirming arrangements	52
	25 A conference call	54
	26 Language review 4	56
Commercial phone calls	27 Placing an order	58
	28 Solving problems	60
	29 Complaining and handling complaints	62
	30 Selling on the phone 1	64
	31 Selling on the phone 2	66
	32 Language review 5	68
Student A Role plays		70
Student B Role plays		72
Listening scripts		74
Phrase bank		82
Answer key		88

To the student

Why *Telephone English*?
Students who need English for business or their professional lives often request help with English on the telephone. This is because telephoning is one of the most important types of communication in the world of work. It is also one of the most difficult areas of communication because we can't see the other speaker and so listening is especially important.

Who is the book for?
You are a learner of English at pre-intermediate to intermediate level and you make and receive telephone calls in English for your work and travel. You have to deal with regular calls such as getting information or arranging to meet. You might also have more difficult calls such as a complaint from a customer or a discussion in a conference call. You want to improve your English on the phone but you also want to be more confident and to communicate more effectively. The book can be used for self study or with a teacher as part of a course.

What does the book include?
- Twenty-seven practice units
- Five language review units
- Role plays for extra practice in class
- Phrase bank of key phrases for telephoning
- Answer key to all the exercises
- CD and listening script

How should I use this book?
Look at the contents page and you will see that the book is divided into five sections. Start with the first section which presents all the essential phrases. After that, you can complete each unit in order or choose units that will help you with the types of calls you make most frequently. The listenings on the CD accompany each unit but you might also want to listen to the CD on its own. This is a good way to review the language.

How are the practice units organized?
Each unit normally begins by listening to a phone conversation. Then it practises the words and phrases you'll need to make or receive a call. The 'Listen and respond' task at the end of many units is your chance to try out the phrases you've learnt in an authentic situation. If you're using the book with other students, you can also use the role plays at the back for extra fluency practice.

The phrase bank
This section summarizes the language you'll need for telephoning. You'll use it during lessons or at home to complete exercises, for reference during role plays and at work when you're planning a call.

General tips
- Plan your call. Make notes on what you want to say and write out important phrases or questions.
- Practise what you are going to say before you call. Do you need to speak more slowly?
- As you make calls, write down any new expressions you hear and add them to the phrase bank.
- If the speaker talks too quickly, don't be afraid to ask them to slow down.
- At the end of a call, summarize what you have agreed so that you can confirm you both understand.

To the teacher

What is *Telephone English*?
Telephone English is a book to help your learners to become more effective on the phone. It is aimed at pre-intermediate to intermediate level students, and consists of:

- Twenty-seven practice units
- Five language review units
- Special 'Listen and respond' tasks
- Role plays for fluency
- Phrase bank to provide a quick reference
- Answer key to all the exercises
- CD and listening script

Why *Telephone English*?
Speaking on the phone is one of the most common types of communication for many of our students. It's also one of the most difficult for them. Even students at advanced levels often require extra help with the specific language of telephone English and with building confidence on the phone. A telephone course must also provide plenty of listening practice as this is the language skill that students tell teachers again and again they have difficulty with.

How can you use *Telephone English* in class?
The thirty-two units are divided into five sections. The final unit in each section is a language review and should be completed when the previous units have been studied. It's advisable to start with the first section of the book as this practises most of the key expressions that students will need for short phone calls. The language is graded so you can follow the units in order on longer courses. For shorter courses, where students need help with specific types of calls, select the most relevant units.

Each unit normally begins with a listening to set the context, followed by exercises to present and practise key language. The 'Listen and respond' task at the end of most units is the students' opportunity to try out the phrases before turning to the role plays at the back which accompany most units.

Organizing the role plays
When using the role plays in class it's worth noting the following:
1 <u>Provide time for planning.</u> When students receive their roles, allow time for them to plan what they will say. They can refer back to the relevant unit(s) or find expressions in the phrase bank.
2 <u>Back-to-back.</u> If you can't provide actual telephones to work on in the classroom, sit the students back-to-back to simulate the fact that they wouldn't be able to see the other person in real life.
3 <u>Record students.</u> If possible, record conversations. Students can evaluate their own performances afterwards. With one-to-one it's also useful for you to listen to afterwards and give feedback.
4 <u>Giving feedback.</u> During the role play, monitor the conversations and make notes of any common language problems you hear. Comment on the performances afterwards. One technique is to write any incorrect sentences on the board and ask the class to try to identify the problem. It's also nice to write up some correct or 'good' sentences so that students can see how well they did.
5 <u>Repeat the role-play.</u> Having given feedback it's a good idea to have students repeat the role play and try to improve. This can be done in the same lesson but you might also re-use a role play in a later lesson for review.

1 Answering the phone

A 1 How do you answer the phone? Tick what you do.

1 greet the caller ☐   4 say your department's name ☐
2 say your name ☐   5 say your telephone number ☐
3 say your company's name ☐   6 offer to help the caller ☐

Listen to a telephone call. Three people answer. Tick what they do.

Person 1 (Reception)
greets the caller ☐   says her telephone number ☐   says her company's name ☐
Person 2 (Sales)
says her name ☐   says her department's name ☐   offers help ☐
Person 3 (Vitale Marini)
says his name ☐   greets the caller ☐   offers help ☐

B Read the article. Are these statements true (T) or false (F)?

1 Many nationalities greet people differently on the phone than they do face-to-face. T / F
2 The Spanish are impolite. T / F
3 When an Italian meets you in the street he greets you with the words 'I'm ready'. T / F
4 At work, different nationalities use a similar approach to answering the phone. T / F

How many ways to say hello?

When two people meet in Tokyo they say *konnichiha* which means *hello*. But if they answer the phone, they say *moshi moshi*. Japan isn't the only country to have its own special 'telephone language'. The Spanish say *hola* for *hello* but on the phone they answer *dígame*. Literally translated *dígame* means 'tell me' – but this sounds very rude in English. Similarly, if a caller heard the words: *I'm ready* in London or New York, they'd think this was very strange. They'd ask 'ready for what?'. But in Italy the word *pronto!* means exactly this.

The rules for answering the phone in the international workplace seem to be more universal. Phone a business number and the receptionist is likely to say the name of the company and answer more politely or formally. For example, in English you make the polite offer of help with *How can I help you?* But even this isn't quite as polite as the very formal Norwegian response: *vær so god* literally meaning 'be so good.'

C

1 Underline the correct phrases in *italics* in the call.

RECEPTION	(1) *Tell me/Good morning*. AIC computing.
JOHN	Sales, please.
RECEPTION	One moment.
SALES	(2) *Ready / Hello*. Sales. (3) *Can I help you?/What do you want?*
JOHN	Yes. (4) *Give me/Can I speak to* Vitale Marini, please?
SALES	Certainly. One moment.
VITALE	Vitale Marini (5) *speaking/talking*.
JOHN	Hi Vitale. (6) *I am/It's* John Peterson here.
VITALE	Oh John. How are you?

Listen to the phone call and check your answers.

D

Practise saying telephone numbers.

To help the listener, say telephone numbers in groups and not as one long number. For example: 569 362 is easier to understand with a pause in the middle: *five six nine, [pause] three six two*

For '0' say *zero* or *oh*. For '22' say *two two* or *double two* (NOT *twenty-two*). For example: 0708 567 3309 = *zero seven zero eight, [pause] five six seven, [pause] three three zero nine* or 0708 567 3309 = *oh seven oh eight, [pause] five six seven, [pause] double three oh nine*

Write these phone numbers in the table and practise saying them.

your home number	
your work number	
your mobile	
your office extension	
a colleague's number	
your manager's number	
your country's international dialling code	

E

2 Read 1–3. What do you say?

1. Ask to speak to Vitale Marini.
2. Greet Vitale and say your name.
3. Say how you are.

Listen and respond. Compare your response with the example after the tone.

2 Making and taking calls

A 🔵 3 Listen and answer the questions Yes (Y) or No (N) for each call.

	Call 1	Call 2	Call 3
Does the person who answers know the caller?			
Does the caller want to speak to the person who answers?			

B 🔵 3 Listen again and tick the phrases you hear.

1 Good morning. AIC Computing. ☐
2 Can I help you? ☐
3 Hello. Three double five, double one two. ☐
4 Can I speak to Vitale Marini, please? ☐
5 Can I have your name, please? ☐
6 Who's calling? ☐
7 This is Walter Geiger. ☐
8 Can you put me through to him, please? ☐
9 It's Midori. ☐
10 Hello IT. Louis speaking. ☐
11 This is Silvia at AIC computing. ☐
12 Is Freddie there? ☐
13 What can I do for you? ☐
14 Could I speak to Freddie, please? ☐

C Put phrases 2–14 in the table below.

Answer the phone	Offer help/Ask who's calling
1 Good morning. AIC Computing.	
Ask to speak to someone	**Say who you are**

D 🔵 4 Some English speakers link words ending in a consonant sound and beginning with a vowel sound. Listen to these phrases and link the words.

1 Can I help you?
2 This is Midori.
3 Can I speak to Walter?
4 How are you?
5 Is Eric there?
6 It's Ann at AIC computing.

Listen again and repeat the phrases. Try to link the words.

E When you make a call, it's a good idea to check the other person has time to talk. Complete phrases 1–5 with the words in the box and match them with responses a–e.

| Are   Do   Have   Can   Is |

1 .... this a good moment?
2 .... you busy right now?
3 .... you have a second or do you want me to call later?
4 .... I rung you at a busy time?
5 .... we talk now or later?

a) Sorry, can you call again later?
b) Now is fine.
c) Yes, you have rather. I'm just dealing with something.
d) Yes, it's fine.
e) I am rather. Do mind calling back this afternoon?

1 .... 2 .... 3 .... 4 .... 5 ....

F Walter speaks to a receptionist and then to Vitale. Put their conversation in the correct order. Number the phrases 1–10.

Hello. Can you put me through to Vitale, please? ....
Hi Vitale. It's Walter. ....
One moment Mr Geiger. ....
Do you have a second or do you want me to call later? ....
Good morning. Can I help you? *1*

Certainly. Can I have you name, please. ....
Hello. Vitale speaking. ....
Oh hello Walter. ....
No, now is fine. ....
Yes, it's Walter Geiger. ....

G 🔵 5 Read 1–4. What do you say?

1 Ask to speak to Freddie.
2 Say your name.
3 Greet Freddie and say your name.
4 Say how you are and check Freddie has time to talk.

Listen and respond. Compare your response with the example after the tone.

3 Reasons for calling

A Match the verbs in A with the nouns in B. They are all reasons for calling.

A (Verbs)	B (Nouns)
a) apply for b) arrange c) make d) place e) query f) request	a catalogue a complaint a course an invoice a job an order

a) apply for a job

B 6 Here are six departments in a company. Match them with the reasons for calling in A.

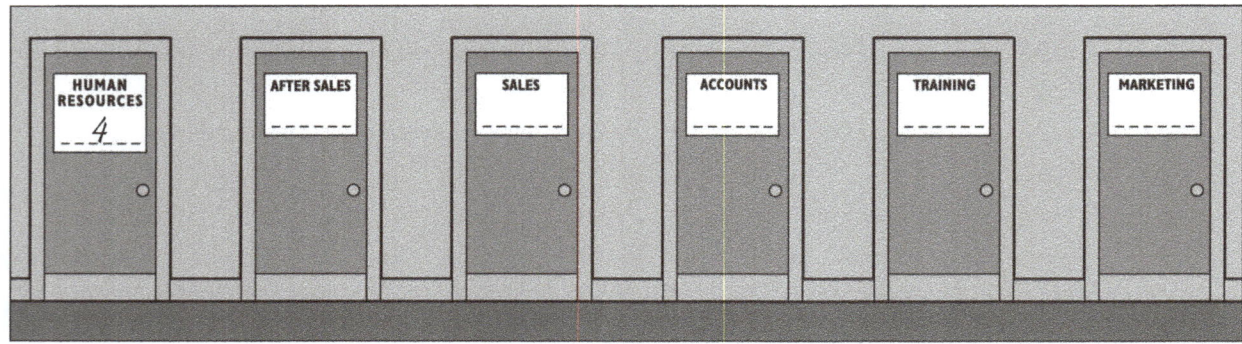

Listen to six calls. Which department is the call for? Write the call number on the door.

C 6 Match three words in the table and complete phrases 1–6 from the listening.

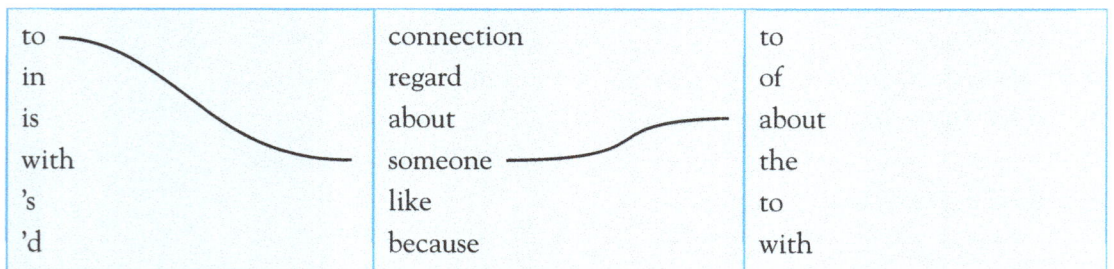

1 Can I speak _to_ _someone_ _about_ receiving a brochure …?
2 I'm calling _____ _____ _____ a payment …
3 The reason I'm phoning _____ _____ some rewritable CDs …
4 Hello. It's _____ _____ the advert …
5 Hi. It _____ _____ English lessons …
6 I _____ _____ change something.

Listen again and check your answers.

D Study this grammar summary. Decide if sentences 1–10 are correct (✓) or incorrect (✗).

> Can I speak to someone about + noun/verb + -ing
> I'm calling about + noun/verb + -ing
> It's with regard to + noun/verb+ -ing
> It's about + noun/verb+ -ing
>
> I'm phoning because of + noun
>
> I'd like to + infinitive
> I'm phoning to + infinitive

1 Is there someone I can speak to about applying for the course? (　)
2 There's someone on the line calling about the new job. (　)
3 I'm calling arrange a meeting. (　)
4 It's with regard to place an order. (　)
5 It's about Natalie, I'm afraid. (　)
6 I'm phoning because of requesting a brochure. (　)
7 I like speaking to someone about the project. (　)
8 I'd like to have a chat. (　)
9 I'm phoning to ask for a catalogue. (　)
10 It's with regard to your request for a brochure. (　)

E 6 Sometimes the person who answers has to connect the caller to another person. Underline the correct word in *italics* in these phrases for connecting the caller.

1 I'll *put/connect* you through …
2 Let me just see if someone's available to *answer/deal* with this…
3 You need to speak to my colleague. I'll *try/transfer* his number for you.
4 I'll just *connect/call* you to the person in charge of this …
5 I'll *transfer/put* you to Silvia.
6 I'll put you *on/back* through to reception

Listen again and check your answers.

F 7 You see a job advert in the local newspaper and want to apply. Read 1–4. What do you say?

1 Give your reason for calling.
2 Say your name.
3 Give your reason for calling.
4 Give your reason for calling.

Listen and respond. Compare your response with the example after the tone.

4 Leaving messages

A 🔊 8 Listen to three calls. Match the calls with these messages.

1	2	3
Rashid – call Gordon.	Gordon called again – it's urgent.	A 'friend' wants to know if you're OK for 6pm tonight!!!

B 🔊 8 Listen again. Which questions does the caller ask? Tick *a, b* or *c*.

Call 1

1 Is Rashid …
   a) with you? ☐   b) there? ☐   c) available? ☐

2 Do you know …
   a) when he'll be back? ☐   b) when he's free? ☐   c) how long he'll be? ☐

3 Can I leave …
   a) my name? ☐   b) my phone number? ☐   c) a message? ☐

4 Please ask …
   a) her to call me back. ☐   b) him to call me back. ☐   c) if he can call me back. ☐

Call 2

5 Can you ask her …
   a) to call me back? ☐   b) if we're still OK for six o'clock tonight? ☐   c) to give me a call? ☐

Call 3

6 Do you know …
   a) how long he'll be? ☐   b) when he'll be back? ☐   c) when he's free? ☐

7 Can you …
   a) say Gordon called? ☐   b) tell him Gordon called? ☐   c) ask him to call Gordon? ☐

C 🔊 8 Match the responses below with questions 1–7 in B.

1 ......   2 ......   3 ......   4 ......   5 ......   6 ......   7 ......

a) I'm afraid not.   c) I'll tell him.   e) Sure.   g) No problem.
b) No, he isn't.   d) I'm not sure.   f) Yes OK.

Listen again and check your answers.

D Read these phrases from the listening and the summary that follows.

> Can you ask him to call me back?   Can you ask her if we're still OK for six o'clock tonight?
> Can you just tell him I called?   Can you say Gordon called?
>
> We ask (or tell) someone to do something. We use an indirect object (*him*, *her*, *them*) after *tell* and *ask* but not after *say*.

Complete these phrases with *tell*, *ask* or *say*.

1 Can you .... her I rang?
2 Can you .... her to call me back?
3 Can you .... I'm arriving at eight?
4 Can you .... them it's urgent?
5 Just .... I'll call again at six.
6 I'd be grateful if you could .... him to call me back.
7 This message is to .... her whether she received the package.
8 It's only to .... them all that we'll start a few minutes late tonight.

E **9** Sometimes in English, we link words and sounds disappear. Listen and compare two speakers saying the same sentence. Then listen and tick the sentence you hear.

Speaker 1: Tell (h)er I called.   Speaker 2: Tell her I called.

1 a) Please ask (h)im to call me. ☐   3 a) Can I leave (h)er my phone number? ☐
  b) Please ask him to call me. ☐   b) Can I leave her my phone number? ☐
2 a) Can she give them my message? ☐   4 a) Is (h)e there? ☐
  b) Can she give (th)em my message? ☐   b) Is he there? ☐

F **10** You call someone, but her colleague answers. Read 1–8. What do you say?

1 Ask to speak to Midori in Marketing.
2 Give your name.
3 Give your reason for calling (to send brochures).
4 Ask when Midori is back.
5 Ask to leave a message.
6 Say you want her to call you back on your mobile.
7 Give your mobile number.
8 Thank the person.

Listen and respond. Compare your response with the example after the tone.

5 Taking messages

A 🔊 11 Listen to someone taking a message. There are three mistakes. Correct them.

Message for:	Herman
Name of caller:	Martha Starligova
Telephone number:	00 39 456 710
Please call back	✓
Urgent	☐
Send brochure	☐
Message:	She'd like you to look at the website. The address is: www.m-sterligova.com/hdm_test66.

B Match reasons 1–10 with phrases a–j from the listening.

Reasons
1 Ask the caller to wait. ....
2 Say you're ready to start. ....
3 Check the spelling. ....
4 Check a difficult spelling. ....
5 Offer to take a message. ....
6 Check the message. ....
7 Give a reason for waiting. ....
8 Check if that's the end of the message. ....
9 Ask for the spelling. ....
10 Find out the reason for the call. ....

Phrases
a) Can I take a message?
b) Sorry, one moment.
c) I'm just getting a pen.
d) OK. Go ahead.
e) As in M-A-R-T-H-A?
f) Can you spell that?
g) Is that S-T-A-R, 'A' as in 'Amsterdam'?
h) What's it in connection with?
i) I'd better read that back to you.
j) Anything else?

C 🔊 12 Listen to people spelling five names. Write them.

1 ....
2 ....
3 ....
4 ....
5 ....

D Make your own list of words you can use to check spelling. They might be the names of famous places, countries, animals or familiar objects. Choose anything that's easy to remember and easy to understand. For example:

A as in 'apple'. B for 'Berlin'.

Practise spelling names 1–5 from C. Use your list to clarify the spelling.

E Here are words for saying email and website addresses.

| @ = at   . = dot   / = slash   _ = underscore   - = hyphen |
| sterligova = all lowercase   STERLIGOVA = all uppercase |

In the telephone call, Martha says the website www.m-sterligova.com/htm_test66.
like this: *www, dot, m, hyphen, sterligova, dot, com, slash, htm, underscore, test, six, six, dot*

Write these email and website addresses and practise saying them.

your work email address	
your home email address	
your company's website	
your favourite website	

F 🔊 13 Listen to a call and write the message.

Message for:	Martha
Name of caller:	
Telephone number:	
Please call back	☐
Urgent	☐
Send brochure	☐
Message:	

G 🔊 14 Read 1–6. What do you say?

1 Say Martha isn't there and offer to take a message.
2 Say you're ready to start.
3 Ask for the spelling.
4 Check the spelling.
5 Find out the reason for the call.
6 Check if that's the end of the message.

Listen and respond. Compare your response with the example after the tone.

6 Asking the caller to wait

A Do you always answer your phone? Do you stop a conversation to answer the phone? Read the article and find out what other people do.

Can you say 'No'?
Not on the phone it seems …

Why is it that we will say to someone: 'Sorry, I'm busy right now. Can we talk later?' but when the phone rings we stop what we're doing and answer it? We even interrupt our conversations to answer the phone. Our friends can wait, but our phone just won't! When you're busy, remember these simple techniques:
- switch on your voicemail
- ask them to call back again later
- ask someone else to answer and take a message
- give people times when you are free to answer calls
- ignore the phone!

B 🌐 15 Listen to a caller for Doctor Alfonso. How many people does the caller speak to?

Now match the two halves of these phrases for asking the caller to wait.

1. Please hold. ☐
2. Are you OK to wait **a couple of minutes** ☐
3. Just bear ☐
4. I'll be ☐
5. Hang ☐
6. Can you ☐

a) or do you want to call back?
b) I'm putting you through **right now**.
c) give me **a minute or so**?
d) with you in **a second or two**.
e) with me **a moment**.
f) on **a second**.

Listen again. Tick the phrases you hear.

C Use words from the time expressions in bold in C to help you finish these sentences.

1 The report will be ready in a day _____ so.
2 Sorry, the Doctor will be a _____ of minutes. Do you still want to hold?
3 OK. We'd better talk about it right _____ .
4 Sorry to interrupt but I just need a _____ of your time.
5 We're expecting the results in a week or _____ 's time.
6 I promise it'll only take a _____ . Or two at the most.

D 🌐 15 When a caller has to wait, we often describe what is happening with the present continuous form of the verb. For example:

Hang on a second. I'm just **getting** a pen …

Complete sentences 1–9 in the present continuous with the verbs in the box.

| not/answer   come   deal   look   open   put   ring   run   work |

1 Please hold. I _____ you through right now. ☐
2 My other phone _____ . I think it's the office. Sorry, let me get this. ☐
3 Hang on a second. I _____ for his extension number. ☐
4 Sorry, he _____ (his phone). ☐
5 Maybe he _____ down in the laboratory. ☐
6 One second. I _____ just _____ the document on the computer now. ☐
7 Don't hang up! They _____ into the room right now. ☐
8 I'll be with you in a second or two. I _____ just _____ with something. ☐
9 Sorry, my battery _____ out. Let me call you back later. ☐

Listen again and tick the sentences you hear.

E 🌐 16 You work in sales. Your colleague Malcolm needs a price on your computer. Read 1–6. What do you say?

1 Answer the phone.
2 Offer Malcolm help.
3 Ask Malcolm to wait – open the document.
4 Ask Malcolm to wait – look for the price.
5 Offer more help.
6 Say goodbye.

Listen and respond. Compare your response with the example after the tone.

7 Asking for repetition and clarifying

A Do these pairs of sentences mean the same thing or something different? Write (S) same or (D) different.

1. Speak up please./Speak more loudly, please. ( )
2. Speak more slowly, please./Please hold a moment. ( )
3. I didn't catch that./I couldn't hear that. ( )
4. I couldn't hear you I'm afraid./I didn't understand what you mean. ( )
5. Can you read that back to me?/Can you take a message? ( )
6. Let me read that back to you./Let me just check I've got that. ( )
7. Would you mind repeating that?/Can you call me back? ( )
8. Sorry, you've lost me./I didn't understand you I'm afraid. ( )

B Complete sentences 1–10 with these pairs of verbs.

| be + speak   got + read   hear + try   mean + know   need + write   say + catch |
| speak + hear   speak + repeat   spell + be   understand + mind |

1. I'm not sure if I ……………… . Would you ……………… repeating it?
2. Please ……………… up. I can't ……………… you very well.
3. Can you ……………… that again? I didn't ……………… the last part.
4. Sorry, that ……………… too fast for me. Can you ……………… more slowly?
5. Please ……………… your surname again so I can ……………… sure.
6. I'm sorry, I still don't know what you ……………… . Is there anyone in your office who ……………… Spanish?
7. I think I've ……………… it but let me just ……………… it back to you.
8. Sorry, I don't ……………… English very well. Can you ……………… it?
9. Perhaps you ……………… to email me, in case I didn't ……………… it down correctly.
10. I can't ……………… you properly. You'd better ……………… calling again.

C 🔊 **17** Listen to the end of a call. The information has mistakes. Listen and correct them.

> Engineer Eskola.
> Arrives on 13th July.
> From Tampere on flight AS 335.
> Plane lands at 3.15.

D 🔊 **17** Here are six techniques you can use to clarify information on the phone. Listen again and tick the techniques the speakers use.

1 Read the information back to the caller. ☐
2 Translate certain words. ☐
3 Say numbers in different ways (eg *fourteen* or *one – four*). ☐
4 Clarify spelling with words (eg 'A' as in 'Amsterdam'). ☐
5 Ask questions. ☐
6 Send an email with the information to confirm. ☐

E 🔊 **18** Listen to these sentences from the call. <u>Underline</u> the information which is stressed. See example 1.

1 <u>Engineer</u> <u>Eskola</u> is <u>arriving</u> on the <u>thirteenth</u> of <u>July</u>.
2 So that's the end of July.
3 And he's coming from Tampere on flight AS three, three, five.
4 Not 'AS'. 'AF'. 'F' as in 'Finland'.
5 And did you say he leaves at three fifteen or lands at three fifteen?

Listen again and repeat the sentences. Remember to stress the important words.

F 🔊 **19** You give details to a colleague about Engineer Eskola's visit. Your colleague reads these details back to you. Correct the information. Read 1–5.

1 Engineer Eskola arrives at the factory at eight o'clock.
2 He has a breakfast meeting with the Managing Director.
3 He leaves on Tuesday.
4 He flies back to Finland from the City airport.
5 His flight number is BA 661.

Listen and respond. Compare your response with the example after the tone.

8 Ending the call

A 🔊 20 Listen to the end of some calls. What happens? Tick *a*, *b* or *c*.

1. The caller dialled
   a) the wrong extension. ☐
   b) the operator. ☐
   c) the wrong number. ☐

2. The caller arranged
   a) a meeting. ☐
   b) to meet a colleague next week. ☐
   c) to meet a friend after work. ☐

3. The caller left a message on
   a) a client's voicemail. ☐
   b) a supplier's voicemail. ☐
   c) a friend's voicemail. ☐

4. The caller
   a) checked flight information. ☐
   b) booked a restaurant. ☐
   c) reserved train tickets. ☐

5. The caller
   a) gave a wake-up call. ☐
   b) made a sales call. ☐
   c) made a social call. ☐

6. The caller
   a) complained about a product. ☐
   b) enquired about a product. ☐
   c) apologized for a product. ☐

7. The caller
   a) had a bad line. ☐
   b) had an argument. ☐
   c) called a wrong number. ☐

B 🔊 20 Listen again and complete these phrases for ending the call.

1. _____ bye.
2. Must _____ . Got another meeting!
3. _____ at seven.
4. Thanks for _____ .
5. _____ to hearing from you.
6. Thanks very _____ .
7. Is there _____ I can help you with today?
8. Sorry I'll have to _____ you there. I'm expecting another call.
9. Thanks for your _____ .
10. It's been _____ talking to you. _____ .
11. _____ can I expect to hear from you?
12. Speak to you _____ in a minute.

C Categorize phrases 1–12 in B.

Say goodbye	1
Give reason for ending	
Refer to future contact	
Thank the other person	
Offer help	

D Match phrases 1–9 with responses a–i.

1 I think I've got the wrong number. Sorry to have bothered you. ....
2 Thanks very much for your help. ....
3 Sorry, I must go now. ....
4 Bye. Have a good weekend. ....
5 Don't forget to give me a ring on Friday. ....
6 Nice talking to you. ....
7 Give my regards to Sheila. ....
8 Don't worry. I'll give her your message. ....
9 So we'll expect you on Thursday. ....

a) Don't worry. I won't.
b) That's OK. No problem.
c) Nice talking to you too.
d) You too. Bye.
e) That's right. Looking forward to it.
f) Thanks.
g) Not at all. Is there anything else I can help you with today?
h) And to Martin and the kids.
i) Yes. Me too.

"Thank you for calling. Please hold until you hang up."

9 Language review 1

A Tenses

Underline the correct verb form in *italics*.

1 Who's *calling/call*?
2 Hi, Walter. This *was/is* Vitale.
3 Sorry, Walter. Have I *rung/rang* you at a bad moment?
4 *I'm calling/I'll call* about an advert in the newspaper. Can I speak to someone?
5 Can you say Gordon *called/calls*?
6 I *be/'ll be* with you in a second.
7 I'll have to stop you there. We*'re expecting/expected* a call any moment.
8 It's *been/being* nice talking to you.

B Phrasal verbs

Match the words in A and B to make phrasal verbs. Then, replace the underlined phrases in sentences 1–9.

A	B
bear call hang hold pass put run slow speak	back down on on out through up up with

1 I'm <u>connecting you</u> now. *putting you through*
2 I'll <u>return your call</u> in a minute. ....
3 Every time I call, she <u>puts the phone down</u>. ....
4 Just <u>wait for</u> me a second. ....
5 Please <u>don't speak so fast</u>! ....
6 My mobile battery <u>is low</u>. ....
7 <u>Wait</u> while I see if he's in. ....
8 It's a bad line. Can you <u>talk more loudly</u>? ....
9 I'll <u>give her</u> your message. ....

C Requests

Write in the missing word in each request.

1 Can I h............ your name?
2 Could you s............ that for me?
3 Can you g............ me your number?
4 Can I h............ you?
5 Could you c............ again later?
6 Can I a............ what it's about?
7 Can I l............ a message?
8 Can we t............ now or later?
9 Could you s............ I called?
10 Can you t............ them I rang?

D Collocations

Complete this information about a telephone answering service. <u>Underline</u> the best verb in *italics*.

Business Extension – Part of your company

Does your business need a little extra help with customers on the phone? Don't keep your callers waiting? (1) *Put/Give/Make* Business Extension a call. We can (2) *do/make/take* incoming calls and (3) *answer/deal/speak* them as if we are part of your business. We're even able to (4) *respond/say/answer* to specific call enquiries such as basic price offers.

And you only pay for the time you use us. That means if your phone rings in the middle of a meeting you can simply (5) *change/divert/turn* the call to us at any time.

Make your day. (6) *Do/Ring/Make* that call today!

Business Extension on 0800 600 600

E Pronunciation

Some of the words and letters of the alphabet below have the same vowel sound. Put them in the table below. See the example.

A bye do E H I me P Q read take through time U wait Y

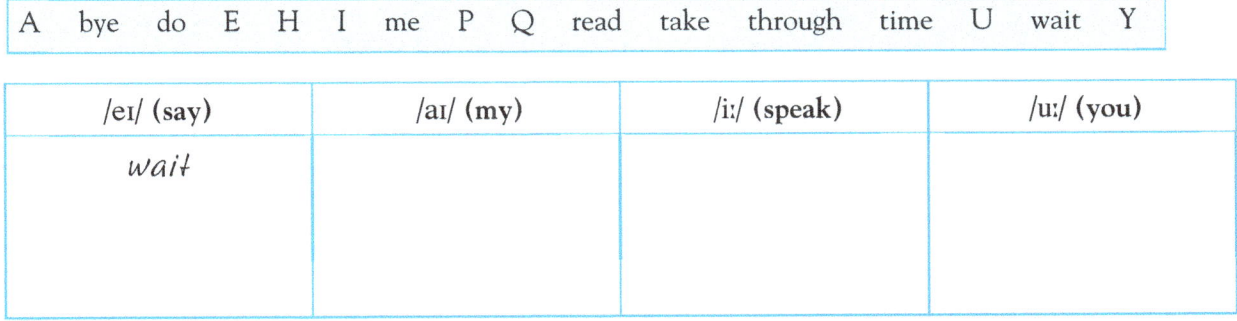

/eɪ/ (say)	/aɪ/ (my)	/iː/ (speak)	/uː/ (you)
wait			

Check your answers in the answer key.

10 Booking hotels and restaurants

Booking a hotel

A 🔊 21 Listen to a guest booking a room at the Tivoli Hotel. Complete the booking form.

B 🔊 21 Complete the hotel receptionist's requests and offers with these phrases. Listen and check.

Can I have	Can I take	How many
How may I help	Is that a	Is there
When is that for	Would you like	

Tivoli hotel — BOOKING FORM

NAME:
NUMBER OF NIGHTS:
DATES:
TYPE OF ROOM:
CREDIT CARD:
CARD EXPIRY DATE:
CONTACT NUMBER:

1 .... you today?
2 .... nights is that for?
3 .... exactly?
4 .... single or a double room?
5 .... the card number?
6 .... a contact number?
7 .... confirmation in writing?
8 .... anything else I can do for you today?

C 🔊 22 Listen to some sentences and circle the date you hear.

1	13th	30th	4	08/08	09/08
2	5th	15th	5	20/12	25/12
3	1/5/78	31/5/78			

Practise saying dates. Answer these questions.

1 When is your birthday?
2 When did you join your present company?
3 When does your credit card expire?
4 When is your next holiday?
5 What's your favourite date of the year?

Booking a restaurant

D Mr Zhou is booking a table at a restaurant called Renoir's. Read the conversation below and complete the questions.

Hello, Renoir's. How may (1) .... ?
I'd like to book a table please.
Certainly. When is (2) .... ?
Wednesday 11th.
Can I (3) .... ?
Mr Zhou.
Can you (4) .... ?
Z-H-O-U.
How many (5) .... ?
A table for two.
Is that (6) .... ?
Smoking, please.
What time is that for (7) .... ?
Eight o'clock.
Fine. So that's a table for two on Wednesday 11th at eight o'clock. Is there (8) .... ?
No. That's everything thanks.
We look forward to seeing you then. Goodbye.

E 🔵 23 To say a word correctly in English, it's important to know how many syllables it has and which syllable has the main stress. Listen to some days of the week and months. Write the number of syllables and mark the stressed syllable. Listen again and repeat the words.

<u>Sun</u>day (*2*)

Monday ( ) Tuesday ( ) Wednesday ( ) Thursday ( ) Friday ( ) Saturday ( )

January ( ) February ( ) April ( ) July ( ) August ( ) September ( )

October ( ) November ( ) December ( )

Three of the months are missing above. They only have one syllable. What are they?

F 🔵 24 Listen and respond. You and your work colleagues want to take the manager out for her birthday at Renoir's. You telephone to book a table. Look at the picture to answer the restaurant's questions.

Begin the conversation with the phrase: *Hello, I'd like to book a table, please.* **Compare your response with the example after the tone.**

11 Booking transport

A 🔵 25 Listen to two phone calls. What type of transport does the woman book in each call? Now complete these phrases from the first call with the words below.

a   an   any   many   much   some

1 I'm calling for .... information about trains to Atlanta.
2 Are there .... more trains leaving this evening?
3 Is there .... overnight train?
4 How .... trains are there tomorrow?
5 I'd like to book .... sleeper ticket.
6 How .... does it cost?

Listen again to the woman booking the train ticket and check your answers.

B There are some differences between American English and British English. Match the American vocabulary on the left with the British vocabulary on the right.

1 (telephone) booth ....   a) mobile phone
2 baggage room ....   b) left luggage room
3 desk clerk ....   c) motorway
4 freeway ....   d) reception
5 front desk ....   e) receptionist
6 one way (ticket) ....   f) return
7 round trip (ticket) ....   g) single
8 subway ....   h) tube/underground
9 cell phone ....   i) kiosk

C 🔵 25 Read the different ways to say the time on the clocks below. Then listen again and tick the ways the speakers say the times.

☐ ten (minutes) past one   ☐ twenty-seven minutes to   ☐ (a) quarter past eleven
☐ one ten am   two (in the afternoon)   ☐ eleven fifteen
                                ☐ thirteen thirty-three   ☐ fifteen minutes past eleven

D Read this summary of prepositions of time.

> **Prepositions of time**
> *on* + day, date, special days (eg *Christmas Day*)
> *by* + time, day, date, month, year
> *in* + month, season, year, part of day (eg *the morning*), period of time (eg *an hour*)
> *at* + time

Are the prepositions of time in these sentences correct (✓) or incorrect(✗)?

1 The overnight train leaves at midnight. ( )
2 It leaves in thirteen forty-five. ( )
3 Can you pick me up by half an hour? ( )
4 I need to be at the station by eleven thirty at the latest. ( )
5 I'd like to book a table on Christmas Eve. ( )
6 I normally go on holiday at the summer. ( )
7 Our annual conference is always in the autumn. ( )
8 Your flight's at eleven so you need to check in by nine at the latest. ( )
9 If you leave a message for him now, he'll get it on Monday. ( )
10 He arrives in the thirty-first. ( )

Complete these sentences for your next trip.

1 Hello, I'd like to book tickets for a trip in ....
2 I want to travel on ....
3 My first meeting is at .... so I need to arrive by ....
4 Could I have a taxi to pick me up in ....

E 🌐 26 You want to book a train ticket. Read 1–8. What do you say?

1 You want a train ticket to Warsaw.
2 Say you want to travel this afternoon.
3 Book the midday train.
4 You want first class.
5 You want a single ticket.
6 Ask the price.
7 Give your credit card number
8 Say goodbye.

Listen and respond. Compare your response with the example after the tone.

12 Dealing with telephone problems

A 🔵 27 **Tick the problems you sometimes have on the phone.**

1 Your phone runs out in the middle of a conversation. ☐
2 There's a lot of noise around you. ☐
3 You ring the wrong number. ☐
4 You can't hear the other person. ☐
5 The other person speaks too quickly. ☐
6 You can't understand the other person's English. ☐
7 You get poor reception on your mobile. ☐

Listen to five problem calls. Write the number of the call under the type of problem in the table.

Problem on the line	Problem using a mobile	Problem with dialling
Call:	Call:	Call:

B 🔵 27 **In each call, one person describes the problem. Complete these phrases with the letters a, e, i, o or u in the adjectives.**

1 It's a really b......d line.
2 It's too n.........sy.
3 I must have got the wr......ng number.
4 My battery's very l......w.
5 The line just went d............d.

Listen and check your answers.

"It's for you."

C To add emphasis we use words called modifiers such as *too* and *really*. Complete these phrases and underline the correct word in *italics*.

1 It's a *really/too* bad line.
2 The reception is *very/absolutely* terrible from the train.
3 I need to recharge my mobile. The battery's *totally/very* low
4 I can't hear. The traffic's *absolutely/too* loud.
5 Sorry, it's *too/such* noisy here today.
6 This line is *such/so* poor.
7 This is *so/such* a terrible line. I can't hear a thing.

D 27 Listen to the five calls in section A again and tick (✓) the actions the speaker suggests.

	Call 1	Call 2	Call 3	Call 4	Call 5
Speak up					
Call back straight away					
Call back later					
Hang up					
Try a different number					

E Re-order the words to make suggestions for solving the problems.

1 sorry you up speak can?
2 the down let's phone put
3 calling try later again
4 me call you let back five in minutes
5 him try 376 on extension
6 email about it sending how me by?
7 up ring the hang and other number

13 Recorded information and phone menus

A 🔊 28 Listen to six automated messages. Which message wants you to …

a) leave a message? ....
b) wait? ....
c) hang up? ....
d) press a number? ....
e) call back? ....
f) call a different number? ....

B Automated information often uses formal language. <u>Underline</u> the formal words in *italics*.

1 Please select one of the following *options/choices*:
2 Please *put the phone down/replace the handset*.
3 Sorry, I'm *unable to/can't* take your call *at the present moment/right now*.
4 We apologize for the *wait/delay*.
5 Please dial *the following/this* number.
6 I'm afraid all our lines are *currently busy/busy now*.

C 🔊 28 Complete the automated messages with sentences 1–6 in section B.

Message 1
The number you are calling has been changed.

....

....

Oh four five, two nine five, oh four oh six.

Message 2
Thank you for calling our cinema customer hotline.

....

....

For details of our films, press one. To book tickets, press two.

Message 3
Sorry, the number you have called has not been recognized. You have not been charged for this call.

....

....

Message 4
Thank you for calling Interstate Finance.

....

....

Please try again later.

Message 5
Due to the high volume of calls, you are currently being held in a queue.

....

....

Your call is important to us.

Message 6
Hello, this is Mack Jones' office.

....

....

Speak after the tone.

Listen again and check your answers.

D We often use imperative verbs in automated and recorded messages and to give instructions. Complete these instructions with an imperative from the box below.

| dial   hold   pick   press   put   select   speak   switch   try |

1 .... two to talk to one of our operators.
2 .... zero for an outside line.
3 All our lines are busy. .... again tomorrow.
4 Please .... after the tone.
5 .... up the receiver.
6 .... in a coin.
7 Please .... off all mobile phones during the flight.
8 .... one of the following options.
9 Please .... All of our operators are busy.

E 🌐 28 Recorded messages are easier to understand when the speaker uses pauses between information. Listen to message 1 and message 2 again. In message 1, notice how the speaker pauses where you see / . In message 2, mark / where the speaker pauses.

Message 1
The number you are calling has been changed. /
Please dial the following number. /
Oh four five, / two nine five, / oh four / oh six. /

Message 2
Thank you for calling our cinema customer hotline.
Please select one of the following options:
for details of our films, press 1; to book tickets, press 2.

F Write your own message by completing these phrases.

Hello. This is ....
I'm afraid I'm ....
Please speak after the tone or call me on ....
Thanks for ....

Now, mark the pauses in your message and practise reading it. Finally, record your message and play it back. Is it clear? Will the listener be able follow your instructions?

14 Leaving voicemail messages

A 🔊 29 Listen to Stephan leaving a message on Bernard Lalo's voicemail. Why is he calling? What are his contact details?

B Add phrases a–j to the flow chart for leaving a message.

a) I work for …
b) You can reach me every day between three and six.
c) Give me a ring. My number is …
d) Speak soon.
e) We met at a conference.
f) Call me at the office.
g) I'm in the … department.
h) Just calling to say …
i) It's in connection with …
j) Or I'll try calling again tomorrow.

1	Introduce yourself	It's … This is … My name's …
2	How you know the person	Your name was given to me by … You/A colleague suggested I call you.
3	Give reason for calling	It's just to let you know … I'd like more information on …
4	Give contact details	You can contact me on … Call me on my mobile. It's …
5	Give availability	I'll be in all day/around until … I won't be in this afternoon so try me again tomorrow.
6	Give alternative	I'll maybe get/catch you later.
7	End message	I look forward to speaking to you. Thanks very much./Bye./See you.

C **29** Number these sentences from the message in the correct order. Use the flow chart in B to help you.

a) Hello, Bernard. My name's Stephan Bougin. I work for Hankel SA in Bern. __1__
b) Or I'll try calling you again tomorrow. _____
c) Look forward to speaking to you. Goodbye. _____
d) Sorry I didn't call sooner but it's been busy since I got back. _____
e) You suggested I call you at some stage to discuss a few ideas. _____
f) You can contact me on 00 41 758 6178. That's 00 41 758 6178. _____
g) You might remember that we met at a conference in February in Lyon. _____
h) Anyway, it's just to let you know I'm interested. _____
i) I won't be in this afternoon but you can normally reach me between nine and twelve. _____

Listen again and check your answers.

D Think of a colleague or client. Imagine you are leaving a voicemail message and complete this message in your own words.

Hello _____ .
My name's _____ .
I work for _____ in _____ .
You might remember that we _____ .
You suggested I call you to _____ .
You can contact me on _____ .
I won't be in this afternoon but you can normally reach me _____ .
Or I'll try calling you again _____ .
Look forward to speaking to you. Goodbye.

Record your message and listen to it. Is it clear?

15 Language review 2

A Countables and uncountables

Underline the correct word in *italics*.

1 We don't have *some/any* tables left this evening.
2 I'd like *a/some* round-trip ticket please.
3 Could you give me some *information/informations*?
4 It's too *many/much* money. I'm afraid I can't afford it.
5 I'm sorry but I only have *a little/few* time left.
6 I don't know how *many/much* times I've called today!
7 There *is/are* still a lot of seats on that flight.
8 I'd like to book *any/some* taxis for tomorrow.

B Phrasal verbs

Complete the phrasal verbs in this telephone conversation.

YVES   Hello? Claire?
CLAIRE Hi Yves. Just bear (1) .... me a second. OK. Where are you?
YVES   On the train to the airport.
CLAIRE Sorry, you're breaking (2) .... How was the meeting?
YVES   Sorry, I can't hear you. Can you speak (3) .... ?
CLAIRE The meeting? How was it?
YVES   Hold (4) .... a moment Claire. We're going to get cut (5) .... My battery's about to run (6) .... Let me call you (7) .... from the airport.

C 'Just'

We often use the word 'just' on the phone. Add the word 'just' to these sentences.

I'm ⁁ looking for my pen. *just*

1 It's to let you know I'll be back at three.
2 It's a quick call to confirm our meeting.
3 Can you email me in case?
4 I'm calling to say …
5 Could you give me his number?
6 I'm afraid I'm rather busy now.
7 You only caught me. I was about to leave.
8 I was speaking to him last week.
9 I'll be with you in a second.
10 Please leave me your number.
11 I wanted to check the prices in your brochure.
12 A single please.

D Collocations

Complete this questionnaire with these missing verbs.

| do | have | make | pass on | spend | take | take |

Now do the questionnaire. Are you a telephone addict?

Time Management on the phone

We can communicate instantly around the world. It's cheaper than flying and quicker than writing. But we also (1) .... more time than ever talking – modern managers are telephone addicts. (2) .... this questionnaire to test yourself. Tick your answers.

	always	sometimes	never
1 Talk to telemarketers and sales people.	☐	☐	☐
2 (3) .... calls twice because you forgot to say something.	☐	☐	☐
3 Stop for the phone when you're (4) .... a meeting.	☐	☐	☐
4 (5) .... a message on any piece of paper.	☐	☐	☐
5 Forget to (6) .... messages to colleagues.	☐	☐	☐
6 (7) .... work at home because of all the calls at work.	☐	☐	☐

If you tick 'always', give yourself 3 points, 2 points for 'sometimes' and 1 point for 'never'. A score of more than 12 out of 18 means you are a 'telephone addict'. You probably need to manage your time on the phone more effectively.

E 30 Pronunciation (Understanding fast speech)

Listen to some phrases. How many words do you hear? Note that contracted forms such as *I've, she's, they'll* count as one word only: *I'll put you through* = four words

You hear the phrases twice. Write the number of words.

1 ....   6 ....
2 ....   7 ....
3 ....   8 ....
4 ....   9 ....
5 ....   10 ....

16 Sounding friendly and polite

A Read the article. Why is it important to smile?

BODY LANGUAGE – EVEN ON THE PHONE

Is it one of those days when the phone just won't stop ringing? By call number four you still answer the phone with a friendly, polite 'Good morning, how can I help you?' But four hours later, twenty calls later and you've lost your smile. You must finish the report for your boss and now – with all these calls – you'll have to work late tonight. So if that telephone rings one more time, don't hang up, don't scream 'Yes!' at the poor caller. Take a deep breath and smile. I know the caller can't see you, but a smile makes your voice sound friendly and polite, a smile makes you feel better and it makes your colleagues in the office feel better.

B 🔵 31 Listen to some expressions on the phone. Is the speaker smiling? Circle the speaker's face.

| 1 ☺ ☹ | 3 ☺ ☹ | 5 ☺ ☹ | 7 ☺ ☹ | 9 ☺ ☹ |
| 2 ☺ ☹ | 4 ☺ ☹ | 6 ☺ ☹ | 8 ☺ ☹ | 10 ☺ ☹ |

C 🔵 32 Listen to these phrases in B. The speaker always sounds friendly and polite.

1. Good morning. Can I help you?
2. I'm very sorry, but he's away today.
3. Can I help?
4. Good morning, Berry Technologies.
5. I don't know when he'll be back.
6. One moment. I'll put you through.
7. Can I take a message?
8. I'm just looking for a pen.
9. Speak to you soon.
10. Goodbye.

Listen again and repeat the phrases. Remember to smile and sound friendly and polite.

D We can also sound more friendly and polite because of the words we use. For example, the first sentence here is less friendly than the second.

1 ☹ Carlsen International.   2 ☺ Carlsen International. How can I help you?

Add words from the first phrase in bold to complete the second friendly and polite phrase.

1 ☹ **What's your name?**
   ☺ Sorry, could I have your _____ ?

2 ☹ **Who do you want to speak to?**
   ☺ Who would you like _____ ?

3 ☹ **She's in a meeting.**
   ☺ I'm afraid _____ .

4 ☹ **He's talking to someone.**
   ☺ One moment. He's just _____ .

5 ☹ **Do you want to wait?**
   ☺ Would _____ like _____ hold?

6 ☹ **What's it about?**
   ☺ Can I ask _____ it's in connection with?

7 ☹ **Wait! I need to find a pen.**
   ☺ Sorry, I'm just looking for _____ .

E In the call below, rewrite A's responses to sound more friendly and polite.

A: Carlsen International.
A: *Good morning. Carlsen International. How can I help you?*

1 B: Hello. Can I speak to Collette please?
   A: **What's your name?**   A: _____

2 B: Mr Zhi-Wei Chiu.
   A: **She's out.**   A: _____

3 B: Oh. Well is Zoran there?
   A: **He's talking to someone.**   A: _____

4 B: Oh dear.
   A: **Do you want to wait?**   A: _____

5 B: No. It's OK. Could I leave my number?
   A: **OK. I'll take a message.**   A: _____

6 B: It's zero, zero …
   A: **Wait! I need to find a pen. Yes?**   A: _____

17 Planning a call

A Read some information about planning telephone calls for sales people. Match headings 1–7 with paragraphs a–g.

1 What questions might the other person ask? ....
2 When is a good time to call? ....
3 Who do you need to speak to? ....
4 What are your objectives? ....
5 What phrases will help you? ....
6 What will you say if you can't get through? ....
7 What will you say if you get an answer machine or voicemail? ....

a	It may seem a stupid question, but we often don't know the name of the person we need. The first rule is to find out as quickly as possible. If you have to, call and ask to speak to 'the person in charge of …' And make sure you use the person's proper title. Calling someone 'Mr' when they are 'Ms' or asking for 'Mrs' when they prefer 'Dr' is a bad start.
b	In the evening most people have been working all day and are having dinner or getting the kids ready for bed. Similarly, someone who works nights won't appreciate being woken in the middle of the day. What is after lunch for you might be when your best client in Japan is normally leaving work.
c	Is it to get information, give information, to convince, to confirm, to arrange or all of these? List what you want from a call – and what the other person might want in return.
d	The person you need might be out or maybe he or she just doesn't want to take any calls today. Ask the person who answers when is a better time to call, or if there is anyone else who can help you.
e	You might decide not to say anything. Few people will return a sales call. But a short brief 'Hello' message with a number they can get you at will be a nice reminder.
f	Understand the other person. What will their objections be? Why aren't they likely to agree? Can you offer them an alternative? This is an essential stage in planning a call.
g	Phone calls can be stressful and it's easy to forget key information. If you're selling a product, list its features and benefits so you can read them out. When talking in a foreign language, write down words or expressions you'll need, and practise saying them before you call.

B **Think about your last call in English.**

1 Did you plan the call?
2 What time of day did you call? Was it the best time?
3 Who did you need to speak to? Did you get through to them or did you speak to someone else?
4 What were the objectives of the call? Did you achieve them?
5 What questions did the other person ask? Could you answer them?
6 What phrases did you use?

C **Plan your next telephone call in English. Complete the plan below.**

Who am I calling?

Best time of day to call?

If that person isn't available, is there anyone else I can speak to?

Objectives of the call?

Questions the other person might ask?

Useful phrases:

What will I say if I have to leave a message?

18 Telephone manner

A 'Telephone manner' is the way we communicate on the telephone. These three jobs all require a good telephone manner. Match the job titles with the job adverts below.

a) Telephone interviewer
b) Telesales agent
c) Customer care telephonist

1 ....
To represent a well-known bank with responsibility for telephoning current and potential customers with details of our financial services and products. Excellent <u>communication</u> skills required with the <u>ability to persuade</u>.

2 ....
A <u>friendly and polite</u> telephone manner is essential to this key service role. The responsibilities of handling everyday enquiries and queries also require the <u>ability to listen</u> and a sometimes <u>sympathetic</u> person.

3 ....
To conduct market research over the phone with members of the public and bank customers. You need to be <u>out-going</u> and have strong <u>interpersonal skills</u>.

B 33 Match the <u>underlined</u> skills and qualities for the three jobs to definitions 1–7.

1 relationships between you and other people ....
2 sociable and friendly ....
3 deal with and talk to people ....
4 people like you and you are never rude ....
5 caring and concerned about people ....
6 make someone agree with you ....
7 not interrupt and show interest in what other people say ....

Now listen to Sally dealing with a caller. What is Sally's job?

C 🌐 **33** In the conversation, Sally shows interest and understanding. Read sentences 1–9 from the listening and tick what Sally says next: *a* or *b*. Then listen again and check your answers.

1 Caller: I have a bank account with your bank.
   a) Right. ☐
   b) Really? ☐

2 Caller: And I'm calling about a mistake on my account.
   a) I see. ☐
   b) Oh dear. ☐

3 Caller: I seem to have paid the same amount twice this month.
   a) When? ☐
   b) OK. ☐

4 Sally: Before we begin I just need to ask you a few details.
   a) Is that OK? ☐
   b) Right. ☐

5 Caller: The number is 022 335 367.
   a) What was it? ☐
   b) That's great. ☐

6 Caller: It's 45 Hensell Street.
   a) That's fine. ☐
   b) Good. ☐

7 Sally: You said it was this month?
   a) Is that right? ☐
   b) Are you sure? ☐

8 Caller: I pay it by direct debit.
   a) Yes. ☐
   b) Right. ☐

9 Caller: This month it went out twice.
   a) I understand. ☐
   b) That's very unlikely. ☐

D Match functions 1–7 with responses a–g.

1 Show you're listening.
2 Show you understand.
3 Show surprise.
4 Show sympathy.
5 Show you have the information.
6 Check you understand.
7 Check the caller agrees.

a) Oh dear.
b) Is that right?
c) Right./OK./Uh-huh.
d) I see./I understand.
e) That's fine./That's great.
f) Really?
g) Is that OK?

E 🌐 **34** A caller wants information on her bank account. Read 1–8. What do you say?

1 Answer, say your name and offer help.
2 Show you're listening.
3 Show you understand.
4 Explain you need the customer's details and check the caller agrees.
5 Ask for the account number.
6 Show you have the information and ask for the first line of the address.
7 Ask for the caller's surname.
8 Thank the caller.

Listen and respond. Compare your response with the example after the tone.

19 Small talk

A 🔵 35 'Small talk' is informal conversation about things which are not usually about work. Are these statements true (T) or false (F) in your country?

1 Small talk is an important part of a phone call. T / F
2 We only make small talk at the beginning of a call before discussing work and not at the end. T / F
3 Small talk on the phone helps to build good relationships with colleagues and customers. T / F

Listen to the beginning and end of a telephone conversation between Midori and Diana. Number the seven stages of the call in the correct order. Notice that one stage is repeated.

Make small talk. ....
Introduce the reason for calling. ....
Greet the other person. ___1___
Make small talk. ....
End the call. ....
Ask how the other person is. ....
End the reason for calling. ....

B Match these phrases to the seven stages of the call in A. Write the stage number next to the phrase.

Hi, Diana. It's Midori. ....
How old are the kids now? ....
Actually, the reason I'm calling is… ....
Anyway I must go. ....
Sorry, I didn't recognize your voice! How are you? ....
Do you fancy coming to stay? ....
It's in connection with… ....
We might take a holiday next year. ....
We really must speak again soon. Bye. ....

C 🌐 35 It's important to show you are listening on the phone and to show interest. Listen again and write in the missing words in these extracts.

MIDORI How old are the kids now?
DIANA Five and seven. They're both at school.
MIDORI (1) .... ?

MIDORI So Nick's in Europe.
DIANA Actually, that's one of the reasons I'm calling. He wants to visit you while he's there.
MIDORI (2) ....

MIDORI It'll be great to see him. Don't you fancy coming too?
DIANA I'd love to, but I can't.
MIDORI (3) ....
DIANA I know, but I'm so busy at the moment.
MIDORI (4) .... !

DIANA So how about we come and visit then?
MIDORI That would be (5) ....
DIANA OK. Talk to Nick about it when he comes. He doesn't think we can both leave the office or the business will collapse.
MIDORI (6) ....

DIANA Anyway I must go. It's been good to talk again.
MIDORI (7) .... We really must speak again soon. Bye

D Think of an old friend or colleague you speak to on the phone. Complete these small talk phrases for you to use.

1 We haven't spoken since ....
2 How are .... ?
3 Are you busy .... ?
4 When are you coming to .... ?
5 We really must ....

20 Formal and informal

A Match the less formal verbs on the left with the more formal verbs on the right.

1	ask for	a)	receive
2	ask	b)	reserve
3	need	c)	request
4	get	d)	assist
5	give	e)	require
6	say sorry	f)	inform
7	tell	g)	apologize
8	book	h)	enquire
9	help	i)	verify
10	check	j)	provide

B Read these pairs of phrases. The first in bold is less formal and more direct. The second phrase is more formal and less direct. Complete the second phrase with any of the words in the first phrase.

Example:
Morning. Jim speaking. Good _morning_ . This is _Jim_ Westermann _speaking_ . How can I help you?

1 **Is Kozma there?** Hello. Could I speak to ...., please?
2 **It's about an advert.** .... with regard to ....
3 **I'm from Bell Inns.** .... calling on behalf of ....
4 **Can I leave a message?** Would you mind taking .... ?
5 **Just tell him I called.** Do you think you could let .... know that ....
6 **Nice to hear from you.** It's so .... again.
7 **Say hello to Richard for me.** Please give my regards .... Mr Arrowsmith.
8 **Give me a ring next week.** Could you .... a call again .... ?
9 **So when are you calling again?** .... do you think I can expect to hear from .... ?
10 **Sorry, she's busy.** I'm .... but .... unavailable at the moment.
11 **Sorry for interrupting.** I'm so .... to bother you.
12 **Call me back.** I'd be grateful if he would return my ....
13 **See you then.** I look forward to .... ing ....
14 **I must get on.** I'm sorry but .... go now.
15 **Thanks for your time.** I really appreciate you giving me ....
16 **Speak soon. Bye.** We'll .... again .... Good ....

C 🔊 36 **When we need to get information on the phone we can sound more formal and polite by changing direct questions into indirect questions.**

> What is his name? → Do you know what his name is?
> What do you do? → Can you tell me what you do?
> When have you used the hotel? → I was wondering when you have used the hotel?

Change direct questions 1–6 into the indirect questions asked by a market researcher.

1   Would you be prepared to answer a few questions?
    I was wondering if you .... to answer a few questions?
2   How many times have you used Bell Inns in the last six months?
    Do you know how many times .... Bell Inns in the last six months?
3   What was the reason for your visit?
    Could you tell me .... for your visit?
4   What do you think of our hotels?
    I'd like to find out .... of our hotels?
5   Could you choose your answer from one of these six categories?
    I'd be grateful .... your answer from one of these six categories.
6   How do you rate the quality and friendliness of staff in a Bell Inn?
    I was wondering .... the quality and friendliness of staff in a Bell Inn?

Now listen to the market researcher and check your answers.

D 🔊 37 **You are a market researcher for Bell Inn restaurants. Read 1–5 and ask the questions on the screen, using the phrases in brackets.**

1   Introduce the call.
    (Good morning. I'm calling on behalf of
    Bell Inns and I'd be grateful if …)
2   Ask question 1.
    (Do you know how … ?)
3   Ask question 2.
    (Could you tell me what … ?)
4   Ask question 3.
    (And finally, I was wondering if … ?)
5   Thank the customer.

Listen and respond. Compare your response with the example after the tone.

1   Use of the hotel restaurants in the last six months:
    never ☐   once ☐   twice ☐
    three times ☐   more than three times ☐

2   The quality and friendliness of restaurant staff:
    excellent ☐   very good ☐   good ☐
    satisfactory ☐   not satisfactory ☐   poor ☐

3   Did you have dinner … ?
    alone ☐   with business colleagues ☐   with friends ☐

21 Language review 3

A Imperatives

Read these guidelines for new employees answering the telephone. Match the two halves of the sentences.

1 Answer the call promptly ....
2 Greet all callers with a smile ....
3 Identify yourself ....
4 Speak clearly ....
5 Listen attentively ....
6 Avoid talking with anything in your mouth ....
7 If the caller has a problem, ...
8 Ask the caller if you can put him/her on hold ....
9 Learn the procedure ....
10 When taking messages ....

a) by the second or third ring.
b) with the correct volume and speed.
c) sound concerned and sympathetic.
d) for transferring calls.
e) and respond to show you're listening.
f) such as gum or sweets.
g) if you need to speak to a colleague.
h) which they'll hear in your voice!
i) use the official forms.
j) and your department.

B Modal verbs

Complete this phone conversation with these modal verbs.

| can't   could   have to   must   should   will   would |

DIANA   Hi Midori. It's Diana.
MIDORI Oh hello! I didn't recognize your voice. I (1) .... remember the last time we spoke. It (2) .... be over two years ago.
DIANA   That's right. The reason I'm calling is that I (3) .... visit Tokyo next month on business.
MIDORI Great. We (4) .... get together.
DIANA   Actually I wanted to ask if I (5) .... possibly stay with you for a couple of nights?
MIDORI Sure. That (6) .... be great. When exactly?
DIANA   Well I'm not sure yet but I (7) .... call you when I know the exact date …

C 'How' questions

Complete the 'How' questions.

1 How l .... is it since spoke?
2 How a .... you and the children?
3 How a .... we visit you next week?
4 How m .... free time do you get?
5 How m .... nights is that for exactly?
6 How w .... your flight?
7 How f .... is the hotel from the airport?
8 How o .... do you play golf?
9 How m .... I help you?

D Verbs + prepositions

Underline the correct preposition in *italics* after the verb.

1 I'm enquiring *about/for/to* an order we placed two weeks ago.
2 I'd like to apologize *with/for/of* my colleague.
3 I want to ask *for/to/with* a new brochure.
4 I'm really interested *for/about/in* the job.
5 We look forward *for/to/at* the meeting.
6 It's just a quick call *about/of/by* next week.

E Direct and indirect questions

Rewrite these indirect questions as direct questions.

1 Could you tell me what time the flight lands?
   What _____ ?
2 I was wondering if I could borrow your mobile?
   Could _____ ?
3 I'd like to know if Yukiko is there, please.
   Is _____ ?
4 I'd be grateful if you'd try his number.
   Would _____ ?
5 Do you know when she'll be back?
   When _____ ?

F ⏺ 38 Pronunciation (Intonation)

Listen and mark the intonation ↘ or ↗ on the words in **bold**.

1 Can I **help** you?

2 Please speak after the **tone**.

3 Is that **right**?

4 Please call me back **on** three five one, two five nine.

5 It's three **five**, six **one**, four five **two**.

Telephone skills   47

22 Making appointments

A 🌐 39 Erich Binder is arranging a conference call with four people. Listen to his conversation with Cheng Ying and answer the questions.

1. Is this Erich's first conversation with Cheng Ying?
2. Why is Erich changing the appointment?
3. Does Erich want the appointment sooner or later?
4. What does Cheng look at?
5. Which day isn't good for Cheng?
6. What day and time do they agree on?
7. How will Erich confirm the appointment?

B 🌐 39 Boxes a–j contain words or phrases (with the same meaning) that complete sentences 1–10 below. Match boxes a–j with sentences 1-10.

a) How about Are you free on Can you make	b) fix arrange agree	c) 're free can make it 're available
d) tied up busy unavailable	e) are you thinking of? do you have in mind? do you want it?	f) postpone it move it back put it back
g) best convenient OK	h) fine great good	i) sound good? suit you? look OK?
j) The appointment is So that's We can confirm		

1. I'm calling to ..*b*.. another time.
2. Michel and Ana are .... this week.
3. Do you mind if we .... to next week?
4. Which day ....
5. Does Wednesday ....
6. .... Thursday?
7. Which would be .... for you?
8. We .... after lunch.
9. That sounds ....
10. .... Thursday at two o'clock.

Sentences 1–10 are from the conversation between Erich and Cheng. Listen again. Which words from a–j do you hear?

C Rewrite these sentences so the second means the same as the first.

1. Which day would you prefer?
   When would be .... ?
2. I'm afraid, I can't make it on Tuesday.
   .... suit me, I'm afraid.
3. I need to postpone our interview.
   I need to put ....
4. Why don't we say at three?
   How .... ?
5. I was thinking of the day after.
   I had the day after ....
6. I'm afraid I won't be able to come on the first.
   I'm sorry but I can't ....
7. Anytime next month sounds fine.
   I'm free ....
8. Thursday at two is confirmed.
   So that's ....

D Read a telephone conversation between Erich and Ana. Underline the less formal words or phrases in *italics*.

ERICH   Hi Ana. (1) *It's me./This is Erich*. It's about (2) *arranging/fixing* a time for this conference call with Cheng Ying. I've just spoken to him and he can (3) *make/attend* the meeting on Thursday at ten our time. Is that going to be (4) *convenient/OK* for you?

ANA   I'm (5) *unavailable/busy* in the morning. Can we (6) *put it back/postpone it* to next week?

E 🔵 40 You arranged a meeting with Cheng and Ana on Tuesday. Ana wants to postpone it. Telephone Cheng to make a new appointment. Read 1–8. What do you say?

1. Give your reason for calling.
2. Explain about Tuesday.
3. Suggest Friday.
4. Suggest next Monday.
5. Suggest the morning.
6. Suggest ten thirty.
7. Confirm the day and time.
8. Say thanks and say goodbye.

Listen and respond. Compare your response with the example after the tone.

23 Inviting people

A 🔵 41 Listen to a telephone conversation between a man and a woman. Who invites who?

<u>Underline</u> the correct verb form in *italics* to make invitations.

1 Would you like *to have/having* a drink? ☐
2 We'd like *to come /coming* over for lunch. ☐
3 How about *meet/meeting* for dinner? ☐
4 Why don't you *join/joining* us at the restaurant? ☐
5 Do you fancy *play/playing* golf at the weekend? ☐

Listen again and tick the sentences you hear.

B How many invitations can you make from the words in this table?

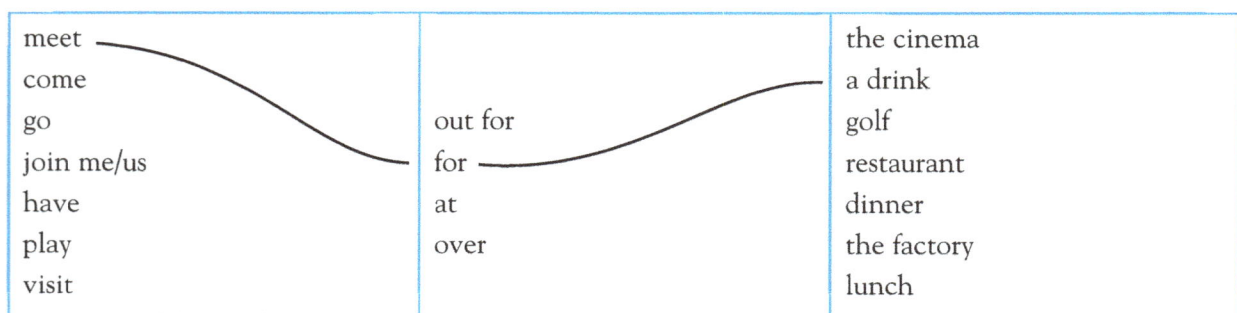

Complete these phrases for inviting with any of the words in the table.

1 Would you like to .... ?
2 We'd like you to .... ?
3 How about .... ?
4 Why don't you .... ?
5 Do you fancy .... ?

C 🔵 41 Listen to the conversation again and complete the phrases below for responding to an invitation.

Accepting an invitation
I'd love to.
That sounds nice.
(1) .... would be great.
(2) .... that very much.

Declining an invitation
Thanks very much but …
(3) .... love to but …
(4) .... of you but …

D Read these sentences and complete the rules for prepositions of place.

> **Prepositions of place**
> I'll be **in** Copenhagen.
> I'm staying **at** the Imperial Hotel.
> We're going **to** the theatre that evening.
> I'm **on** the fifth floor.
>
> 1 Use .... after verbs of movement (*go, travel, fly*).
> 2 Use .... with a room, a meeting, a country or city.
> 3 Use .... for a trip, holiday or the floor of a building.
> 4 Use .... for websites, buildings, places of work (but not *home*).

Are the prepositions in sentences 1–10 correct or incorrect? Put a tick (✓) or a cross (✗) and write the correct preposition.

1 I spent the weekend at work. (✓) ....
2 Visit our website in www.ludco.com. (✗) *at*
3 I'm afraid I'm not on the office at the moment. ( ) ....
4 Would you like to meet at reception? ( ) ....
5 Let's meet at the second floor. Take the lift. ( ) ....
6 I fly to Berlin tonight. ( ) ....
7 Sorry, he's in a meeting at the moment. ( ) ....
8 How about joining us for dinner at the restaurant? ( ) ....
9 Why don't you meet me later on for a drink to the hotel bar? ( ) ....
10 I normally get to home by six in the evening. ( ) ....

E 🌐 42 Your friend Raymond calls to invite you out tonight but you are going out to the cinema. Read 1–9. What do you say?

1 Answer the phone.
2 Ask how he is.
3 Say you're fine.
4 Decline the invitation.
5 Accept the invitation.
6 Invite your friend to the cinema tonight.
7 Say you're meeting at 8pm.
8 Tell him it's the cinema on Geld street.
9 Say goodbye.

Listen and respond. Compare your response with the example after the tone.

24 Confirming arrangements

A 🔊 43 Melissa Omiotek works for a Public Relations agency. She is organizing the opening of a new art exhibition. Roger Molinas, the art gallery manager calls her about the final arrangements.

Listen to the call and write in the three missing times in Melissa's schedule.

> Thursday
> (1) .... - 5.00pm: catering company to set up
> (2) .... : opening
> 7.00 - (3) .... pm: press conference

B 🔊 43 Listen to the conversation again. Are these statements true (T) or false (F)?

1 Melissa arranged for the catering company to arrive in the afternoon. T / F
2 The catering company is at the gallery now. T / F
3 The catering company will have left by the time the guests arrive. T / F
4 Melissa doesn't know if the artists and the journalists will be in the gallery at the same time. T / F
5 Melissa decides to ring the journalists. T / F

C 🔊 43 Listen again. Complete these sentences from the listening with the missing verbs.

1 .... you .... the food?
2 Yes, I .... the catering company a month ago.
3 But what time .... they .... ?
4 We don't .... until six thirty …
5 I think they .... by about five.
6 .... the journalists .... the artists at six thirty or later?
7 I think I .... them.

Now match the verbs in sentences 1–7 with these tenses.

Past simple .... 2 .... Future simple ....
Present perfect .... Future continuous ....
Present simple .... Future perfect ....
Present continuous ....

D   Put the verbs in brackets into the correct tense.

1   Hello, I .... (phone) about the new exhibition next week.
2   Not everyone .... (finish) eating by the time the journalists get here.
3   She .... (not/call) me back yet this morning. Do you think she knows?
4   Don't worry! They .... (be) here on time.
5   What time does the gallery normally .... (close)?
6   We .... (hold) the press conference as soon as they arrive.
7   .... you .... (reserve) the restaurant afterwards?
8   By six thirty the guests .... all .... (arrive).
9   We'll have the press conference while the guests .... (look) at the paintings.
10 I promise that the artists .... (not/be) late!

E   44 Two groups of journalists from France and Japan are visiting the gallery. Melissa emails this schedule to Roger but he doesn't receive it. You are Melissa. Roger telephones you.

To: Roger
From: Melissa

Dear Roger
I've divided up the journalists because there are too many for the gallery AND we'll need translation into French and Japanese so I think it's better to have two separate groups. Will this work?

French Group
10.00–10.15 Welcome by Roger
10.15–11.00 Look at paintings
11.00–12.00 Interview artists
12.00–13.00 Buffet reception

Japanese Group
10.45–11.00 Welcome by Roger
11.00–11.45 Look at paintings
12.00–12.45 Interview artists
12.45–13.45 Buffet reception

Melissa

Listen and respond to Roger's five questions using the information in the email above. Compare your responses with the examples after the tone.

25 A conference call

A 🔘 45 Pema manages a call centre in Bangalore which receives calls from the UK. She wants to provide training for the staff. She has asked a training company in the UK to provide help. Listen to the conference call between Pema, Mira and Simon, who runs the training company, and answer the questions.

1. What is Mira in charge of?
2. What does Simon think the course should be about?
3. Does Mira agree? What does she want to include on the course?
4. Do the employees at the call centre need the most help with speaking or listening?
5. What does Pema promise to do at the end of the meeting?

B Match the purpose on the left with the phrases from the listening on the right.

1	Check the participants.	a)	Mira is in charge of …
2	Check the volume.	b)	I agree.
3	Welcome a participant.	c)	Are you there Simon?
4	Introduce a participant.	d)	Let's speak again in … (two weeks)
5	Explain the purpose/aim.	e)	Can you hear me?
6	Ask for an opinion.	f)	What do you think?
7	Express an opinion.	g)	Thanks for joining us today.
8	Agree.	h)	The reason for …
9	Disagree.	i)	Mira wants to say something …
10	Agree with a suggestion.	j)	So, to summarize …
11	Let someone else speak.	k)	I like that idea.
12	Show understanding.	l)	I see what you mean.
13	Summarize.	m)	I don't agree.
14	Check people's actions.	n)	Mira, you're going to …
15	Refer to a future conference call.	o)	I think that …

C Complete this discussion from the next conference call with words from the phrases in B.

PEMA   Hello. Simon? Are you (1) _____ ?
SIMON   Yes
PEMA   Can you (2) _____ me OK?
SIMON   It's fine.
PEMA   Great. Thanks for (3) _____ me and Mira.
SIMON   Hello Mira.
MIRA   Hi Simon
PEMA   OK. So the (4) _____ for this conference is to finalize plans for the course.
        OK? Mira wants to say something.
MIRA   Did you receive my report Simon?
SIMON   Yes and I see what you (5) _____ about the problem of accents and listening.
PEMA   I agree. So I (6) _____ the course needs lots of listening and pronunciation.
MIRA   Yes, I like that (7) _____ .
SIMON   No problem. I can email a course programme later today.
PEMA   That's great. When do we run the course? (8) _____ do you think?
SIMON   Next month?
MIRA   I'd need to check the schedules. We might need two or three groups.
PEMA   Mira can you check and let's (9) _____ again about the dates next week.
SIMON   Pema, we can arrange that by email.
PEMA   I (10) _____ .

26 Language review 4

A '–ing' or infinitive?

Complete the phrases below with the verbs in brackets. Write the verb in the infinitive or '-ing' form.

1. Thanks for .... (join) us today.
2. I'm going .... (call) him back.
3. I'd love .... (play) golf at the weekend.
4. Do you like .... (play) golf?
5. I'm phoning .... (arrange) an appointment.
6. How about .... (meet) for lunch?
7. Do you fancy .... (come) to the cinema?
8. Would you like .... (have) a coffee?
9. Sorry but I have .... (go) now.
10. Look forward to .... (see) you later.

B Phrasal verb word order

Re-order these phrases with phrasal verbs.

1. put I'll through you. ....
2. can I you back call? ....
3. hang the phone again and up try. ....
4. that back let to me you read. ....
5. he's up I'm tied afraid at the moment. ....
6. this please message on pass. ....
7. with just with second bear me a. ....
8. down me let take your name. ....
9. looking in try up his number the phone book. ....
10. speak you can up? ....

C Prepositions

<u>Underline</u> the correct preposition and complete it with information about you.

1. I usually switch my voicemail on when I leave work *on/in/at* ....
2. You can call me at home *on/in/by* ....
3. Have you visited our website *to/at/on* .... ?
4. The busiest time of day for me is from .... *after/during/to* ....

5   I like to spend my annual holiday *on/in/to* _____ .
6   The battery on my mobile lasts *for/during/after* _____ hours.
7   My office is *on/in/at* _____ floor of the building.
8   In the evening, I usually take visitors and clients *at/to/from* _____ restaurant.
9   The best time of the day to call me is *to/in/on* _____ .
10 We usually have an office party *at/on/during* _____ .

D Common mistakes

These phrases contain a mistake. Re-write the phrases correctly.

1   Hello, I am Marco speaking. _____
2   Is Tuesday suit you? _____
3   I'm really interesting in the job. _____
4   I'm afraid but he's out of the office today. _____
5   I really sorry about this. _____
6   Can you say him I called? _____
7   Sorry but I must to go now. _____
8   I call you back tomorrow. _____
9   I'm agree with you. _____
10 She call in connection with an invoice. _____

E 🔊 46 Pronunciation (Sentence stress)

Listen to these phrases and underline the stressed words.

1   Are you <u>there</u>?
2   Can you hear me?
3   Thanks for joining us today.
4   The reason for this meeting is …
5   What do you think?
6   I see what you mean.
7   I like that idea.
8   Let's speak again soon.

Listen again and repeat.

27 Placing an order

A Here are four people describing problems. Read the text from the Spyline brochure and write the product each person needs to order.

1 ....
"I spend half my day answering calls from sales people. It drives me crazy!"

2 ....
"When I make personal calls at work I think my boss is listening."

3 ....
"He said he would send it by Friday, but I don't know if believe him!"

4 ....
"My boss even calls me at home. I can ask my wife to answer and say I'm out, but it's a problem when she's out."

Spyline

Specialists in telephone equipment for security and detection.

Voice Changer

Don't let them recognize your voice. The 'Voice Changer' fits to any phone allowing you to make or answer calls in a different voice.

Truth Teller

Originally developed by the military, the 'Truth Teller' is now available to security firms and private detectives. Now you can ask questions on the phone and the truth teller will tell you if the person's answer is 100% true.

Call Pass

Only allows callers with a pass code to connect to your phone. Stop those unwanted calls!

Phone Protector

Are you worried someone is listening? 'Phone Protector' stops others from monitoring your private calls.

B 🔊 47 A customer places an order at Spyline. Listen to the call and complete this order form.

ORDER FORM

CATALOGUE NUMBER	PRODUCT DESCRIPTION	PRICE	QUANTITY
(1)	Voice Changer	$586	(2) ....
SL 34 TT	Truth teller	(3) $..................	1
SL 35 CP	Call Pass	$305	(4) ....
(5)	Phone Protector	$315	(6) ....

C 🔊 47 Listen again and complete these phrases for placing an order.

1 I've been looking at your ....
2 I'd like to .... , please.
3 .... two voice changers, please?
4 I .... a Truth Teller …
5 And .... one Call Pass?
6 Oh and one more ....
7 I have a .... about …
8 .... five of those, please.
9 When can I expect .... ?
10 Can I pay by .... ?

D 🔊 48 You want to place an order for some Spyline products. Read 1–10. What do you say?

1 Give your reason for calling.
2 Order the Voice Changers (2).
3 Say the catalogue number (SL 33 V).
4 Order the Truth Teller (1).
5 Say the price ($478).
6 Order the Call Pass (1).
7 Say the catalogue number and price (SL 35 CP/$305).
8 Order the Phone Protectors (5).
9 Ask about the time for delivery.
10 Ask to pay by credit card.

Listen and respond. Compare your response with the example after the tone.

28 Solving problems

A 🔊 49 A customer wants Euro Deliveries to deliver a package. Listen to the call and complete the booking form.

EURODELIVERIES

REFERENCE NUMBER:
COLLECTION TIME:
CONTENTS OF PACKAGE:
DESTINATION:

B 🔊 49 Listen again and match the two halves of the sentences.

1 We're going to ....   a) be too late!
2 The trade fair starts .... b) agents all day.
3 It's going to ....   c) collect it this afternoon.
4 We're meeting ....   d) call you back in about five minutes.
5 I'll ....   e) this afternoon.

C Complete this summary of future forms with sentences 1–5 in B.

For making predictions: *It's going to be too late!*
For timetables or programmed events: ....
For arranged events (eg meetings): ....
For promising action: ....
For a planned future event (or intention): ....

Now <u>underline</u> the correct future form to complete these sentences.

1 A: Can you see me tomorrow at three? B: Sorry, *I'll meet/I'm meeting* someone at three.
2 The timetable says it *leaves/is going to leave* at five.
3 A: Order YY 354 still hasn't arrived. B: *I'll contact/contact* the warehouse and see what's happened.
4 There are lots of people here. I think it's *going to be/'s being* successful.
5 They called to say the delivery was late again. They *cancel/'ll cancel* the contract unless we improve.
6 There's a problem with the shipment. I think the delivery *is/is going to be* late.
7 Sorry, *I'm leaving/I'm going to leave* on a business trip next week. It's been planned for ages.
8 Don't worry. *I'm calling/I'll call* you back straight away.
9 *I'm working/I'm going to work* for a new company as soon as I can.
10 When we start to use it, I think the new system's *going to work/works* much better.

D 🌐 49 Listen to the end of the call to Euro Deliveries again. The Euro Deliveries representative promises to call back in five minutes. What other action does he promise?

Promise 1: ....
Promise 2: ....
Promise 3: *To call back* ....

E We often use the *'ll* form (future simple) to promise action. Match the problems 1–6 with the actions a–f.

1 The package is ready to collect.
2 I can't open the attachment for some reason.
3 Why hasn't our order arrived?
4 What time is the delivery due?
5 Please tell him that my flight is delayed.
6 Did you remember we have a meeting today?

a) I'll call you back in five minutes and let you know.
b) I'll just check in the schedule.
c) I'll send someone immediately.
d) I'll be there in one minute.
e) I'll give him your message.
f) I'll email it again.

F 🌐 50 You work for Euro deliveries. You receive a call from a customer. Read 1–6. What do you say?

1 Answer the phone.
2 Ask for a reference number.
3 Promise to send a courier.
4 Promise to check flight times.
5 Promise to call back to let the caller know.
6 Say goodbye.

Listen and respond. Compare your responses with the example after the tone.

29 Complaining and handling complaints

Complaining

A 🔘 51 Listen to a complaint and complete the notes in the flowchart.

How to complain effectively

Say what the main complaint is

.... was late and incomplete.

Describe what happened

We .... it yesterday and there was only .... the order.

Say what you want

We need them ....

B Complete sentences 1–10 with these irregular verbs in the past simple.

| be   break   buy   cost   get   give   have   make   pay   send |

1 When we opened it, there .... only half the order.
2 I'm calling because one of the items .... as soon as I used it.
3 It's in connection with the software we .... in your shop last week.
4 I .... three hundred pounds to have it fixed and it still doesn't work.
5 We didn't .... anything delivered this morning.
6 What do you mean I don't have a room? I .... a reservation.
7 It .... me a fortune to transport it and you damaged everything inside.
8 I only called this morning about the problem because I didn't .... time yesterday.
9 Your technician .... me a new part but it doesn't fit.
10 Are you sure you .... the replacement?

Handling complaints

C Match the techniques for handling complaints on the left with the phrases from the listening on the right.

1 Show you're listening. ....
2 Show you understand. ....
3 Ask a question to clarify. ....
4 Restate the problem. ....
5 Apologize. ....
6 Propose action. ....
7 Explain action. ....

a) Let me see what I can do about this.
b) Do you have a reference number for it?
c) I see.
d) I'll call our warehouse.
e) So the order was a week late …
f) I'm sorry but …
g) I understand.

D 🔵 52 Another useful technique for handling complaints and keeping customers is to make a follow-up call. Listen to this follow-up call on Mr Sevin's answer machine a week later. Write in the phrases for apologizing.

Hello. This is Mr Sevin. I ⁽¹⁾ .... I'm unable to get to the phone right now. Leave a message after the tone.

Hello Mr Sevin. This is Karl at Moran Machinery. I spoke to you a few days ago about a problem with a delivery. I'm ⁽²⁾ .... for the mistake and I hope you've received the rest of the items. As I say I ⁽³⁾ .... and please ring me if you have any further problems. Goodbye.

E 🔵 53 You work for Moran Machinery. A customer calls to complain. Read 1–8. What do you say?

1 Answer the phone.
2 Show you're listening.
3 Show understanding.
4 Ask for a reference number.
5 Restate the problem.
6 Apologize and propose action.
7 Promise to call the warehouse and call back.
8 Say goodbye.

Listen and respond. Compare your response with the example after the tone.

30 Selling on the phone 1

A 🌐 54 Listen to three parts of a sales call. Which three ways to find jobs do the speakers mention? Listen again and answer questions 1–8.

1. Which department does Mr Morandi work in?
2. Where is the newspaper sold?
3. How many graduates does the company employ per year?
4. Does the website always attract the right people?
5. What does Marco suggest is the problem with other newspapers?
6. What's the free offer this month?
7. What will Marco send Mr Morandi?
8. What else does Marco want to do?

B There are five stages to a sales call. Read sentences a–j from the listening below. Match two sentences to each stage.

a) Advertising in national newspapers is so expensive …
b) How many new graduates do you recruit a year?
c) We have a special feature for our readers next week on careers so your advert would appear on the same page …
d) Good morning, my name's Marco Pani. I'm calling from Student News.
e) So it sounds like you need more quality applicants …
f) This offer also includes free promotion at a careers fair.
g) We're a newspaper which is only sold to students in universities and colleges …
h) Would you mind if I call again later this week?
i) What percentage of applicants come from your website?
j) Well thank you for your time.

C Imagine you are a sales person. Complete these stage one phrases for you.

Good morning, my name's _____
I'm calling from _____
We're a company which _____

D A sales rep is finding out about a customer and his company. Complete his questions (Qs).

1 Q: .... in charge of?
   A: I'm responsible for training and recruitment.
2 Q: .... company do?
   A: We manufacture electronic parts for things like mobile phones.
3 Q: .... employ?
   A: About 500 across Europe and 200 in Asia.
4 Q: .... advertise job vacancies on the Internet?
   A: Because it's cheaper than newspapers.

E The sales rep identifies needs and problems. Match the needs (1–4) with the problems (a–d)

1 Due to the fact that newspaper advertising can be a rather slow process, ...
2 Because newspapers advertising is so expensive, ...
3 To help you with the problem of low quality applications ....
4 With so many unsuitable applicants, ...

a) we provide a more cost effective online recruitment service.
b) it sounds like you need more effective advertising.
c) we recommend careers fairs as a faster way to recruit.
d) our company guarantees a minimum number of high-achieving candidates.

F Re-order these words to make phrases to close the call.

1 you for time thank your ....
2 I mind next you if call would again week? ....
3 forward you again to I look speaking to ....

31 Selling on the phone 2

Dealing with customer enquiries

A 🔊 55 Read this advice for selling on the phone and listen to a customer enquiry. Which rules doesn't the sales rep follow?

Don't lose sales.

FOLLOW THESE BASIC RULES:

a Answer the telephone quickly. Don't leave it more than five rings. If you have to leave it longer, remember to apologize to the customer.
b Start each call with your name, position or department.
c Show you're listening and don't interrupt.
d Find out and use the other person's name early on in the telephone conversation.
e Find out how the customer heard of you.
f Make notes about the caller's enquiry and read back the key points.
g Say exactly what action you will take as a result of the conversation.

B Match phrases 1–10 with the rules in A.

1 Can I ask how you heard of us? ..e..
2 I see. ....
3 Sorry, can I just take down your name? ....
4 Can I just read that back to you? ....
5 I'm sorry to have kept you waiting. ....
6 OK. I'll send you a brochure and then call you early next week. ....
7 Good morning. Customer services. This is Marie speaking. ....
8 So let me just check I've got all your details. ....
9 Did someone recommend us to you? ....
10 I'll pass on this information to my colleague and he'll call you back. ....

C 🔊 56 You work for the company 'Discount Wine' and receive a call. Read 1–8.

1 Answer the phone.
2 Ask for the customer's name.
3 Show you're listening.
4 Ask how the customer heard about your company.
5 Offer to send a brochure or visit.
6 Ask for the address.
7 Read the details back.
8 Say what action you'll take.

Listen and respond. Compare your response with the example after the tone.

Selling to difficult customers

D Customers often avoid sales calls. Complete sentences 1–7 with phrases a–g below.

a) we've used your company before
b) I don't have any budget
c) offer me a cheaper price
d) but we wouldn't be interested
e) I'm not the person responsible
f) Send me a brochure
g) it's very happy with them

1 I'm really sorry but .... left this year.
2 It sounds very interesting. .... and I'll take a look.
3 I'm afraid .... and we weren't happy with the results.
4 Actually .... for that. You'd have to talk to Marek in purchasing.
5 TLX already has a supplier and .... thank you.
6 I'm sure the products are all very good .... at the current time.
7 When you can .... , get back to me. My name's Paul Powers and I'm on extension 3661.

E Read these responses from a sales caller to the customer's sentences in D. What do the words in bold refer to?

1 I'm sorry to hear that, but I think you might find **we**'ve improved.
   the company

2 Well in fact I'm visiting your area next week. I can bring **one** over personally.
   ....

3 Let me talk to my boss and I'll hopefully call **you** back with another offer.
   ....

4 Do you know when **it** will be reviewed for next year?
   ....

5 But you might be interested if **they** were all on special offer for this month only.
   ....

6 OK. Do you know **his** number?
   ....

7 Well, if you ever experience problems with **them** in the future, please give me a call.
   ....

32 Language review 5

A Tenses

Underline the correct verb form.

1. She always *calls/is going to call* at nine o'clock to check I'm here.
2. When we *have opened/opened* the box the items were all broken.
3. *I've just received/I just received* the package and I'm not happy.
4. Sorry, he*'ll just talk/'s just talking* to someone at the moment. Can he call you back?
5. By the time you ring back, Thierry *is finishing/will have finished* lunch.
6. Can I ask how you *hear/heard* of us?
7. Because it's urgent, I*'ll check/will have checked* with the supplier right now.
8. I *am/was* wondering if you could help me with something?
9. Please tell them I *call/called*.
10. The fault is quite serious. I don't think we're *going to have/having* phones until Tuesday at the earliest.

B Questions

Complete these questions.

1. .... is your company based?
2. .... people do you employ?
3. .... percentage of your business is via the Internet?
4. .... your company export?
5. .... department do you work in?
6. .... you in charge of advertising?
7. .... is responsible for your marketing?
8. .... did you join the company?
9. .... you find you spend too much time on the phone?
10. .... you like to speak to my colleague?

Now match these answers a–j with the questions. Write your answers here:

1 ...... 2 ...... 3 ...... 4 ...... 5 ......
6 ...... 7 ...... 8 ...... 9 ...... 10 ......

a) About fifty work for us.
b) Around thirty percent.
c) My colleague.
d) No, I'm not.
e) Four years ago.
f) Yes, to the rest of South America.
g) Yes, more and more.
h) Is he free?
i) IT
j) The headquarters is in Helsinki.

C Wordbuilding

Complete these sentences with a noun form of the word in brackets.

The ___delivery___ (deliver) was late again today.

1 We sell our _____ (produce) all over the world.
2 When can we expect _____ (pay)?
3 It's in _____ (connect) with our order.
4 There's been a _____ (delay) at customs.
5 I'll email it as an _____ (attach).
6 I'd like to book a _____ (fly) to Madrid, please.
7 We buy all our mobiles from a famous _____ (manufacture) in Finland.
8 Could you give me some _____ (inform) on train times, please?

D Linkers

Read these sentences from an interview with a telephone manufacturer. Complete the sentences with the linkers and linking phrases.

| As | As a result | ~~Because~~ | Due to | Hence | In response | Therefore | With so |

1 ___Because___ of customer demands, we're adding new features.
2 _____ many of our customers now changing provider, we're lowering our prices.
3 _____ the fall in home phones, we're introducing a new phone for both home and mobile use.
4 _____ it's more reliable, we'll change.
5 _____ of the rising costs, we can offer you a new package.
6 People want it. _____ we sell it.
7 _____ to market research, we're launching phones in different colours.
8 Production costs have gone up – _____ the rise in prices.

E 🔊57 Pronunciation (Adding emphasis)

Listen to these sentences and underline the stressed word.

1 I'm really sorry for that.
2 I do apologize.
3 I'm afraid I just don't know.
4 Monday will be too late.
5 I'm so grateful for your help.
6 I'd love to join you.
7 That sounds great!
8 We're not very happy with our supplier.
9 I'm sure your products are all excellent.
10 I can bring one over personally.

Listen again and repeat.

Student A Role plays

2 Making and taking calls

Call Louis at AIC Computing. Speak to the receptionist. Say who you are and wait.
Now Louis answers. Say who you are. Check he has time to talk.

3 Reasons for calling

You work in the Human Resources Department of a company. Answer the phone. Take the caller's details.

4 Leaving messages

Call Rashid. Ask when he'll be back. Ask to leave a message: you want him to call you on your mobile.

5 Taking messages

You call Martha but her colleague answers. Leave the following message: you need the report on customer feedback as an email attachment. Give your name, number and email address.

6 Asking the caller to wait

Call and ask to speak to Henri Reiser.

7 Asking for repetition and clarifying

Call your colleague about a visit by a client next week. You want your colleague to meet the visitor at the airport. Give your colleague the following information about the client's arrival:

> Engineer Guidi visits on 30th May
> From Naples on flight AI 116
> Plane lands at 1413.

8 Ending the call

It's very quiet in your office today. Call a colleague and ask if they want to meet for coffee.

10 Booking hotels and restaurants

You ring Renoir's Restaurant. You want a table for six on 15th December at 8.15pm. Two guests smoke.

11 Booking transport

Telephone the train station. Find out times of trains to Berlin and decide when you want to leave. Book two tickets for a train. Find out the price and give your credit card details.

12 Dealing with telephone problems

Call your colleague from your mobile on the train. Explain you will be an hour late for your meeting.

22 Making appointments

Call Mr Francone to arrange a meeting on Tuesday 25th at 3.15. The meeting will be in your office.

23 Inviting people

You have two tickets for Dial 'M' for Murder. Telephone your friend and invite him/her.

24 Confirming arrangements

One of the people in your department is organizing your Managing Director's leaving party. Here is the schedule but you have information missing. Call to confirm the arrangements.

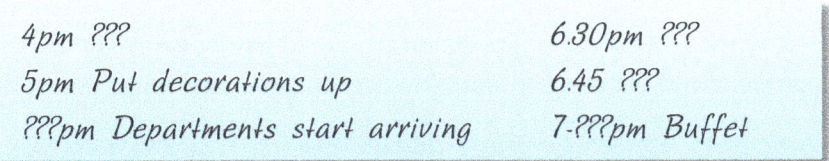

```
4pm ???                           6.30pm ???
5pm Put decorations up            6.45 ???
???pm Departments start arriving  7-???pm Buffet
```

25 A conference call

You are in charge of training at your company. You want to arrange English lessons for staff in the sales department. Call the sales manager to discuss: how many staff? the best time/day?

27 Placing an order

Call your supplier at 'Spyline' and place the order below:

CATALOGUE NUMBER	PRODUCT DESCRIPTION	PRICE	QUANTITY
SL 33 VC	Voice Changer	$586	5
SL 34 TT	Truth teller	$478	2
SL 35 CP	Call Pass	$305	1
SL 36 PP	Phone Protector	$315	10

28 Solving problems

You ordered some brochures for a trade fair in Seattle. They haven't arrived. Telephone the delivery company to find out what they can do.

29 Complaining and handling complaints

You are staying in a hotel. Telephone reception and complain that: the television in your room doesn't work; room service hasn't delivered dinner and you ordered it an hour ago; there aren't any towels in your room.

30 Selling on the phone 1

You run a company called 'Netdesign'. You design websites for companies. Ring a customer. Find out if they have a website and arrange a sales visit.

31 Selling on the phone 2

You saw an advert in yesterday's newspaper for computer printer cartridges. Large orders will receive 20% off if you order before the end of the month. Call the company.

Student B Role plays

2 Making and taking calls

You are the receptionist at AIC computing. Answer the phone and ask for the caller's name. Connect the caller to Louis.

Now you are Louis. Answer the phone. Say you don't have time to talk. Ask the caller to call later.

3 Reasons for calling

You saw a job advert in the paper for the position of trainee manager. You'd like to apply for the job. Call the Human Resources Department and ask them to send you details. Give your name and address.

4 Leaving messages

Answer the phone. Rashid is out of the office today. You don't know when he'll be back. Take a message for him. Take the caller's mobile number.

5 Taking messages

Answer the phone. Martha is out. Take a message for her.

6 Asking the caller to wait

You work in Henri Reiser's office. Answer the phone. Henri is talking on another line. Find out if the caller wants to wait.

7 Asking for repetition and clarifying

Your colleague calls about a visit by a client next week. Write down the information about the client's arrival at the airport.

8 Ending the call

Answer the phone. It's a colleague. You're VERY busy today.

10 Booking hotels and restaurants

You are the manager of Renoir's restaurant. Answer the phone and take a booking. Remember to ask for:

- customer's name?   - number of guests?   - date and time
- a contact number? - smoking or non-smoking table?

11 Booking transport

You work at the train station. Answer the phone and answer the questions about trains to Berlin. Use this travel information. Take the caller's booking. Find out:
- how many tickets   - give price
- which train   - take credit card details

BERLIN TRAINS

Departure times	Arrival times	Price
0835	1315	42 euros
1205	1650	42 euros
1523	1940	37 euros

12 Dealing with telephone problems

You're waiting for your colleague to arrive. You have a meeting with him/her and you can't meet later on. Answer your colleague's call. It's a really bad line.

22 Making appointments

Your are Mr Francone. Your colleague calls to arrange a meeting. You have a day off on Tuesday 25th. You are free at 3.15 on the next day. Find out where the meeting is.

23 Inviting people

Your friend calls and invites you to the theatre. Find out when it is. Accept or decline.

24 Confirming arrangements

You are organizing your Managing Director's leaving party. Here is your current schedule. Your boss calls to confirm the arrangements.

4pm Caterers arrive
5pm Put decorations up
6pm Departments start arriving
6.30pm The Managing Director arrives
6.45pm Speeches and champagne
7-9pm Buffet

25 A conference call

You are a sales manager. The company wants your staff to have English lessons. You have ten staff but they are very busy and some don't want English lessons. The only time for lessons would be after work at 6pm but no-one wants to stay late. Talk to the training manager and try to find a solution.

27 Placing an order

Your work at Spyline. Take a customer's order and complete the order form below:

CATALOGUE NUMBER	PRODUCT DESCRIPTION	PRICE	QUANTITY
	Voice Changer	$586	
SSL 34 TT	Truth teller		
	Call Pass	$305	
SL 36 PP			

28 Solving problems

You work for a delivery company. A regular customer calls with a problem. What action will you take?

29 Complaining and handling complaints

You work in a hotel. A customer calls you with some complaints.

30 Selling on the phone 1

Answer a call from a company which design websites. You don't have a website so you are interested. Arrange for the person to visit.

31 Selling on the phone 2

You work for the 'Print Machine'. You have a special offer on printer cartridges at the moment. Take the customer's details and offer to visit his/her company.

Listening scripts

Essentials

1 Answering the phone

🔵 1

RECEPTION Good morning. AIC computing.
JOHN Sales, please.
RECEPTION One moment.
SALES Hello. Sales. Can I help you?
JOHN Yes. Can I speak to Vitale Marini, please?
SALES Certainly. One moment.
VITALE Vitale Marini speaking.
JOHN Hi Vitale. It's John Peterson here.
VITALE Oh John. How are you?

🔵 2

1 Hello. AIC Computing. Can I help you?/Can I speak to Vitale Marini, please?
2 Hello. Vitale Marini speaking./Hi Vitale. It's John Peterson here.
3 Oh John. How are you?/Fine thanks. And you?

2 Making and taking calls

🔵 3

1
WOMAN Good morning. AIC computing. Can I help you?
WALTER GEIGER Good morning. Can I speak to Vitale Marini, please?
WOMAN Who's calling?
WALTER GEIGER This is Walter Geiger. I'm a friend of Vitale's.
WOMAN One moment.

2
DIANA Hello?
MIDORI Hi. Is that Diana?
DIANA Yes, speaking.
MIDORI Hi Diana. It's Midori.
DIANA Oh hi Midori. I didn't recognize your voice! How are you?

3
LOUIS Hello. IT. Louis speaking.
SILVIA Hi Louis, this is Silvia at AIC computing.
LOUIS Oh hi Silvia. How are you?
SILVIA Good thanks.
LOUIS What can I do for you?
SILVIA Could I speak to Freddie, please?
LOUIS Erm. He isn't at his desk. I'll just ask someone …

🔵 5

1 Hello. AIC Computing. Can I help you?/Can I speak to Freddie, please?
2 Sure. Can I have your name, please?/This is Walter Geiger. I'm a friend of Freddie's./One moment. I'll put you through.
3 Hello. Freddie speaking./Hi Freddie. It's Walter.
4 Oh hi. How are you?/Fine thanks. Have I rung you at a bad moment?/No. It's fine.

3 Reasons for calling

🔵 6

1 - I found your company in the phone directory and I'd like some information about your products. Can I speak to someone about receiving a brochure or catalogue, please?
   - Certainly. One moment. I'll put you through …
2 - Hi. I'm calling in connection with a payment for the last job I did. I still haven't received any money.
   - One moment. Let me just see if someone's available to deal with this …
3 - Hello. The reason I'm phoning is because of some rewritable CDs that we bought from you. I'm afraid there's something wrong with them …
   - Oh I'm sorry. You need to speak to my colleague. I'll try his number for you.
4 - Oh hello. It's with regard to the advert for the post of secretarial assistant in today's paper. It says I can get more information on this number about the vacancy.
   - That's right. I'll just connect you to the person in charge of this …
5 - Hi. It's about the English lessons which are starting next week. Well, do you know if anyone can attend?
   - Sorry. I don't know anything about it. I'll transfer you to Silvia. She might know.
6 - Hello. I placed an order with you this morning and I'd like to change something.
   - Sorry, you've come through to the wrong extension. I'll put you back through to reception and they'll be able to connect you …

🔵 7

1 Hello. AIC Computing. How can I help you?/I'm calling in connection with the job advert in the paper.
2 One moment. Can I have your name, please?/It's Ray Graham./One moment. I'll put you through to Human Resources.
3 Hello. Human Resources./Hello. I'd like to apply for the job in today's paper./I'll just connect you to the person in charge of this.
4 Hello. Job applications./Hello. I'm calling about applying for the job in today's paper.

4 Leaving messages

🔵 8

1
ROSINE Hello. Accounts.
GORDON Hi Rosine. It's Gordon. Is Rashid there?
ROSINE No, he isn't. Err … he isn't at his desk. Sorry Gordon, we think he's in a meeting.
GORDON Do you know when he's free?
ROSINE I'm not sure. I hope he'll be back at eleven because I'm meeting him then.
GORDON Can I leave a message?
ROSINE No problem.
GORDON Please ask him to call me back.
ROSINE I'll tell him.
GORDON Bye.

2
RASHID Hello. Rashid speaking.
MAN Hello, can I speak to Rosine please?
RASHID I'm afraid not. She's out at the moment. Can I help?
MAN Err … no it's OK … err … Can you ask her if we're still OK for six o'clock tonight?
RASHID Yes. OK. Who's calling?
MAN It's a friend. She'll know who it is.
RASHID Bye.

3
ROSINE Hello. Accounts.
GORDON Hello, can I speak to Rashid, please?
ROSINE I'm sorry but he's on another call. Do you want to hold?
GORDON No, it's OK. Do you know how long he'll be?
ROSINE I'm afraid not. Is it urgent?
GORDON Yes. Can you say Gordon called?
ROSINE Sure.
GORDON Is that Rosine again?
ROSINE Yes.
GORDON Oh hello, Rosine. Thanks. Bye.
ROSINE Bye.

🔵 10

1 Hello./Hello. Can I speak to Midori in Marketing, please?
2 Who's calling?/This is Silvia Trevor.
3 Can I ask what it's in connection with?/It's with regard to sending some brochures.

4 One moment … Let me check. I'm sorry, she's out this morning./Do you know when she'll be back?
5 I'm afraid I don't./Can I leave a message for her?
6 Sure. No problem./Can you ask her to call me back on my mobile?
7 OK. Can I have your mobile number, please?/It's oh double seven nine oh, five three nine, double two double nine.
8 That's fine. I'll give her your message. Good bye./Thanks. Bye.

5 Taking messages

11

MARTHA Hello, is Herman there?
MAN One moment. Can I just put you on hold?
MARTHA Yes, OK.
MAN I'm sorry, he's with a client at the moment.
MARTHA Do you know when he'll be free?
MAN I'm afraid I don't. Can I take a message?
MARTHA Thanks. Can you tell him …
MAN Sorry, one moment. I'm just getting a pen. OK. Go ahead.
MARTHA Can you tell him Martha called?
MAN Martha. As in M-A-R-T-H-A?
MARTHA That's right.
MAN And your surname?
MARTHA Sterligova.
MAN Can you spell that?
MARTHA Yes, it's S-T-E-R-L-I-G-O-V-A.
MAN Sorry is that S-T-A-R, 'A' as in 'Amsterdam' or S-T-E-R, 'E' as in 'Egypt'?
MARTHA 'E' as in 'Egypt'. Sterligova.
MAN OK Martha. And has he got your number?
MARTHA Yes, but I'll leave it just in case. It's double 0 39 456 7 double 1 0.
MAN And what's it in connection with?
MARTHA It's about the website. Can you tell him to take a look at it? The website address is: www, dot, m, hyphen, sterligova, dot, com, slash, htm, underscore, test, T-E-S-T, six, six, dot.
MAN OK I'd better read that back to you. It was www, dot, m, hyphen, sterligova, dot, com, slash, 'H' as in 'Hungary', 'T' as in 'Turkey', 'M' as in 'Madrid', underscore, test, sixty-six, dot.
MARTHA That's right.
MAN OK. Anything else?
MARTHA Just if he can call me back.
MAN OK.
MARTHA Thank you very much.
Goodbye.

12

1 Josef Marogg. M-A-R-O-G-G.
2 Dottore Palgimi. That's P-A-L-G-I-M-I.
3 Ms Hansen. H-A-N-S-E-N.
4 That's T-O-I-M-I-T-U-S-J-O-H-T-A-J-A.
5 Senhor Lopo. L, 'O' as in 'Oslo', P, O.

13

TEIXEIRA Hello, is Martha there?
WOMAN I'm sorry she's in a meeting. Can I take a message?
TEIXEIRA Thanks. Can you tell her …
WOMAN Sorry, one moment. I'm just getting a pen. OK. Go ahead.
TEIXEIRA Can you tell her Teixeira called?
WOMAN Can you spell that?
TEIXEIRA Yes, it's T-E-I-X-E-I-R-A.
WOMAN Sorry is that T-E-'I' as in 'Italy' or T-E-'A' as in 'Australia'?
TEIXEIRA 'I' as in Italy.
WOMAN OK. And has she got your number?
TEIXEIRA Yes, but I'll leave it just in case. It's double 0 351 567 double 1 0.
WOMAN And what's it in connection with?
TEIXEIRA I need the report urgently. Please email it. My email is teixlopo, at, lisboa, hyphen, globe, dot, pt.
WOMAN OK, I'd better read that back to you. It was teixlopo all lower case, at, lisboa, hyphen, globe, dot, pt.
TEIXEIRA That's right.
WOMAN OK. Anything else?
TEIXEIRA No that's it. Thank you very much. Goodbye.

14

1 Hello, is Martha there?/I'm afraid not. Can I take a message?
2 Yes, please./OK. Go ahead.
3 Can you tell her Teixeira called?/Can you spell that?
4 Yes, it's T-E-I-X-E-I-R-A./I'd better read that back to you: T-E-I-X-E-I-R-A.
5 That's right./And what's it in connection with?
6 I need the report urgently. Can she email it? /Anything else?/No, that's it. Thank you very much. Goodbye.

6 Asking the caller to wait

15

MALCOLM Good morning. Can I speak to Doctor Alfonso in Research?
WOMAN Please hold. I'm putting you through right now.
MAN Hello. Research?
MALCOLM Hello. Is that Doctor Alfonso's office?
MAN No. Sorry. He works in the office next door.
MALCOLM Oh.
MAN It's OK. Hang on a second. I'm looking for his extension number … Here we are. Let's try this. (pause) Sorry, he isn't answering. Maybe he's working down in the laboratory. Erm … Just bear with me a moment.
DOCTOR Hello?
MALCOLM Doctor Alfonso?
DOCTOR Speaking.
MALCOLM Hello. It's Malcolm.
DOCTOR Oh hello Malcolm … . I'll be with you in a second or two … I'm just dealing with something, sorry to keep you waiting … Listen, Malcolm, are you OK to wait a couple of minutes or do you want to call back?
MALCOLM It's OK. I can tell it's a bad moment. Speak to you later.
DOCTOR Thanks Malcolm. Speak later.

16

1 Hello. Sales department.
2 Hi. It's Malcolm./Hi Malcolm. How can I help?
3 Can you give me the price on item 334?/Just bear with me. I'm opening the document now. OK. Here it is.
4 Great. And what's the price?/One moment. I'm just looking for it. OK, it's five hundred and thirty-six dollars.
5 Thanks a lot./Is there anything else?
6 No that's all. Thanks. Bye./Bye Malcolm.

7 Asking for repetition and clarifying

17

- OK. Let me read that back to you. Engineer Eskola is arriving on the thirteenth of July.
- The thirtieth: three, zero.
- Oh sorry. So that's the end of July.
- That's right.
- And he's coming from Tampere on flight AS, three, three, five.
- Not 'AS' – 'AF'. 'F' as in 'Finland'.
- Oh yes, of course. AF, three, three, five. And did you say he leaves at three fifteen or lands at three fifteen?
- No. He lands at three fifty: five zero.
- Oh OK. Got that. Fine. OK. We'll look forward to meeting him.

19

1 Let me read that back to you. Engineer Eskola arrives at the factory at eleven o'clock./No. He arrives at **eight** o'clock.
2 Oh sorry. And he has a lunchtime meeting with the Managing Director./No, he has a **breakfast** meeting.
3 OK. And he arrives on Tuesday, yes?/No, he **leaves** on Tuesday.
4 And he flies back from Gatwick

airport./No, from the **City** airport.
5 And did you say BA, six, six, one or BE, six, six, one?/BA: '**A**' as in '**Amsterdam**'./OK. Thanks. I think I've got it now.

8 Ending the call

 20

1 - Sorry, but there's no-one of that name works here.
   - Is that Wells and co?
   - No, sorry.
   - Oh I'm so sorry to have bothered you.
   - That's OK. Goodbye.
2 - Sorry. Must go. Got another meeting!
   - OK. See you at seven.
   - Thanks for calling.
3 - … we need fifty more straight away so if you could let me know tomorrow morning I'd appreciate it. My number's zero double seven, three four nine, four six seven six. Look forward to hearing from you. Bye.
4 - Your seat is booked. It leaves from platform five at eight fifteen.
   - Thanks very much.
   - Is there anything else I can help you with today?
   - No that's it. Thanks very much.
5 - Sorry I'll have to stop you there. I'm expecting another call …
   - OK. I wonder if I could call you again in a month's time … just to see if you're still interested?
   - Yes. Ok.
   - Thanks for your time.
   - It's been nice talking to you. Bye.
6 - I'll need to check with my manager and see if we can give you a replacement.
   - When can I expect to hear from you?
   - Tomorrow morning.
   - Good.
   - As I say I'm very sorry about this.
   - That's OK as long as you can change it. Goodbye.
7 - Sorry, I can't hear you very well. Can you speak up?
   - Why don't you hang up and try again?
   - OK. Speak to you again in a minute.

Everyday phone calls

10 Booking hotels and restaurants

 21

- Hello. The Tivoli Hotel. This is Tania speaking. How may I help you today?
- Hello. I'd like to book a room for next month.
- Certainly. Can I have your name, please?
- Mr Zhou.
- Sorry. Can you spell that?
- Z-H-O-U.
- Thanks. And how many nights is that for?
- Just two.
- And when is that for exactly?
- The 11th and 12th of July.
- Is that a single or a double room?
- Well actually it's for me on the first night and then my wife will be staying with me on the next night.
- OK. So a double room on both nights. Will that be OK?
- That's fine.
- And can I have a credit card number to secure the reservation?
- Yes it's a Visa card. It's 6677 3424 0798.
- And the expiry date?
- December 2010.
- OK. And can I take a contact number Mr Zhou?
- Certainly. My mobile's 08993, 8679, 4876.
- Right. That's everything. You have a double room for two nights next week, reference number RF239. Would you like confirmation in writing Mr Zhou?
- No, it's alright thanks.
- Is there anything else I can do for you today?
- No thank you.
- We look forward to seeing you next month and hope you have a nice stay with us.
- Thanks. Goodbye.

 22

1 I need a room for the thirteenth, please.
2 I'm staying until the fifteenth of next month.
3 My last visit here was on the first of May 1978.
4 My credit card expires in September 2008.
5 Sorry, can I change my reservation on the twenty-fifth of December?

 24

RENOIR'S Hello, Renoir's. How may I help you today?/
Hello, I'd like to book a table, please.
RENOIR'S When is it for?/
Tuesday the tenth of April.
RENOIR'S Can I have your name, please?/
Mr Zhou
RENOIR'S Can you spell that?/
Z-H-O-U
RENOIR'S And how many people is that for?/
Six people.
RENOIR'S Smoking or non-smoking?/
Smoking please.
RENOIR'S What time is that for exactly?/
Nine o'clock.
RENOIR'S Fine. Is there anything else?/
No thanks. That's everything.
RENOIR'S We look forward to seeing you then. Goodbye./
Goodbye.

11 Booking transport

 25

1 - Good evening, Central trains. How may I help you?
   - Hello, I'm calling for some information about trains to Atlanta.
   - OK.
   - Are there any more trains leaving this evening?
   - Let me check. No, sorry it looks like you've missed the last one today.
   - Oh dear. Is there an overnight train?
   - There is. It leaves at ten minutes past one.
   - Oh. How many trains are there tomorrow?
   - Just the one. It leaves at thirteen thirty-three.
   - OK. I'd like to book a sleeper ticket on the night train, please.
   - OK. I'll need your name and credit card number.
   - How much does it cost?
   - One-way or round-trip?
   - One-way.
   - That'll be … ninety-four dollars …
2 - Good evening. Fast Cabs.
   - Hello, I need a taxi to take me to the train station.
   - Where from?
   - I'm at eighty-nine Melville Street.
   - What time is that for?
   - How long does it take to the station?
   - About half an hour.
   - Ok. Can it pick me up at a quarter past eleven?
   - No problem. And who is that for?
   - Ms Meier.
   - OK. That's reserved for you Ms Meier.

 26

1 Good evening, Centrum trains. How may I help you?/I'd like a train ticket to Warsaw.
2 OK. When would you like to travel?/Are there any trains leaving this afternoon?
3 Let me just check that. OK. There are two this afternoon. One leaves at midday and the other at a quarter to four./OK, I'd like to book a ticket on the midday train.
4 OK. Would you like a first or second class seat?/First class, please.
5 And is that a single or return?/A single.
6 Right. So that's a first class, single ticket./How much is that?
7 That'll be one hundred and eleven

euros. Can I have a credit card number to guarantee that booking?/Visa, 5445, 6834, 0581, 9064, expiry 06/09.
8 OK. That's reserved for you. Thank you very much. Have a good journey./Goodbye.

12 Dealing with telephone problems

 27

1 - Hello? Hello? Sorry, I can't hear you? It's a really bad line. No. Speak up. Let's put the phone down and try calling again later …
2 - Hello. Oh hi Sara. Yes. Sorry. Sorry, I didn't catch that. Can you speak up? Yes. I'm calling from my mobile outside the station. Look Sara. Let me call you back in five minutes … when I'm inside … yes … it's too noisy here … yes … in five minutes …
3 - Hello. Is Aiko there?
  - Sorry, Aiko doesn't work in this office.
  - Oh sorry to have bothered you. I must have got the wrong extension.
  - No problem. Try Aiko on extension 3166.
4 - Hello. Oh hello. Yeah I made it. It's not bad. It's a four star, but there's a sauna so I thought I might use it later on. Sorry Olga. Let me call you back on the other phone. I'm on my mobile and my battery's very low. I think we're going to get cut off any moment. Yeah, I've got your number. I'll call you straight back.
5 - So what time do you think you'll be arriving?
  - Well my flight lands at three …
  - Hello?
  - Hello, it's me again.
  - Sorry I don't know what happened.
  - No the line just went dead.
  - If it happens again, try my home number.

13 Recorded information and phone menus

28

1 The number you are calling has been changed. Please dial the following number: oh four five, two nine five, oh four oh six.
2 Thank you for calling our cinema customer hotline. Please select one of the following options: for details of our films, press 1; to book tickets, press 2 …
3 Sorry, the number you have called has not been recognized. You have not been charged for this call. Please replace the handset.
4 Thank you for calling Interstate Finance. I'm afraid all our lines are currently busy. Please try again later.
5 Due to the high volume of calls you are currently being held in a queue. We apologize for the delay. Your call is important to us.
6 Hello, this is Mack Jones' office. Sorry, I'm unable to take your call at the present moment. Speak after the tone.

14 Leaving voicemail messages

29

1 - This is the voicemail of Bernard Lalo. I'm afraid I'm unable to answer your call at the moment. Please leave a message after the tone.
- Hello, Bernard. My name's Stephan Bougin. I work for Hankel SA in Bern. You might remember that we met at a conference in February in Lyon. You suggested I call you at some stage to discuss a few ideas. Sorry I didn't call sooner but it's been busy since I got back. Anyway, it's just to let you know I'm interested. You can contact me on 00 41 758 6178. That's 00 41 758 6178. I won't be in this afternoon but you can normally reach me between nine and twelve. Or I'll try calling you again tomorrow. Look forward to speaking to you. Goodbye.

15 Language review 2

30

1 I'll put you through.
2 How are you?
3 It's ages since we spoke.
4 I'll be in all day.
5 Sorry, I can't hear.
6 I must get on.
7 She isn't in today.
8 Could you tell him I called?
9 Do you know when they're back?
10 I'll try calling tomorrow.

Telephone skills

18 Telephone manner

33

SALLY Hello, Sally speaking. How may I help you today?
VADALA Oh hello. My name's Mrs Vadala and I have a bank account with your bank …
SALLY Right.
VADALA And I'm calling about a mistake on my account.
SALLY I see.
VADALA Yes, I seem to have paid the same amount twice this month.
SALLY OK. Before we begin I just need to ask you a few details. Is that OK?
VADALA Yes, that's fine.
SALLY First of all, do you have your account number?
VADALA Yes … the number is 022 335 367.
SALLY That's great. And can you tell me the first line of your address?
VADALA It's 45 Hensell Street.
SALLY That's fine. And finally your surname?
VADALA Vadala.
SALLY And the initial of your first name?
VADALA 'C' for 'Christina'.
SALLY OK Mrs Vadala. Thank you very much. Let's have a look at your account. You said it was this month? Is that right?
VADALA Yes.
SALLY And what exactly was the amount?
VADALA A hundred and fifty euros.
SALLY OK. I'm just looking.
VADALA And I pay it by direct debit.
SALLY Right.
VADALA But this month it went out twice.
SALLY I understand. OK I think I've found it …

 34

1 Hello, Sally speaking. How may I help you today?
2 I'm calling about my bank account./Right.
3 And I'd like to know how much I have in it./I understand.
4 Can you tell me?/Before we begin I just need to ask you a few details first. Is that OK?
5 Yes, that's fine./First of all, do you have your account number?
6 Yes it's 022 335 367./That's great. And can you tell me the first line of your address?
7 45 Hensell Street./That's fine. And finally your surname?
8 Vadala. V-A-D-A-L-A./That's great. Thank you.

19 Small talk

35

MIDORI Hello?
DIANA Hi. Is that Midori?
MIDORI Yes, speaking.
DIANA Hi Midori. It's Diana.
MIDORI Oh hi, Diana. Sorry, I didn't recognize your voice.
DIANA How are you?
MIDORI Fine thanks. And you?
DIANA Good.
MIDORI It's ages since we spoke.
DIANA Yes, it is. Not since the Dublin trade fair two years ago.
MIDORI So how are Nick and the kids?
DIANA They're fine. Nick's away in Budapest.
MIDORI How old are the kids now?

DIANA Five and seven. They're both at school.
MIDORI Really?
DIANA I know.
MIDORI So Nick's in Europe.
DIANA Actually, that's one of the reasons I'm calling. He wants to visit you while he's there.
MIDORI Great …

MIDORI OK. Great. We'll expect Nick to call when he arrives. We can pick him up from the airport if you like.
DIANA No, it's OK. He can take a taxi.
MIDORI It'll be great to see him. Don't you fancy coming too?
DIANA I'd love to, but I can't.
MIDORI That's a pity.
DIANA I know, but I'm so busy at the moment.
MIDORI Me too!
DIANA We employ thirty people now and someone has to run things here! We might take a holiday at the beginning of next year and come over to Ireland, take a tour and visit Nick's parents. So how about we come and visit then?
MIDORI That would be wonderful.
DIANA OK. Talk to Nick about it when he comes. He doesn't think we can both leave the office or the business will collapse.
MIDORI I'll tell him.
DIANA Anyway I must go. It's been good to talk again.
MIDORI Yes. We really must speak again soon. Bye.
DIANA Bye Midori.

20 Formal and informal

 36

- Hello?
- Good morning, I'm calling on behalf of Bell Inns, the hotel chain. To improve the service Bell Inns offers its client we're currently carrying out some market research. You recently stayed at one of our hotels and I was wondering if you would be prepared to answer a few questions?
- Erm, well I suppose so …
- It'll only take a few minutes. And all your answers are treated confidentially.
- OK then.
- Great. Thank you very much. First of all, do you know how many times you have used Bell Inns in the last six months – approximately?
- A couple of times I think. I stayed in one last month and then I visited Seattle in January.
- So twice then.
- Yes, I think so.
- And could you tell me what the reason was for your visit?
- For work. I had business there.
- Fine. Now I'd like to find out what you think of our hotels.
- Yes.
- I'd be grateful if you could choose your answer from one of these six categories. They are excellent, very good, good, satisfactory, not satisfactory and poor. OK?
- Yes, I think so.
- Great. And I was wondering how you rate the quality and friendliness of staff in a Bell Inn between excellent to poor?
- Erm. Fine. Yes, not bad.
- Not bad, so is that good? Satisfactory?
- A bit more than satisfactory.
- So good?
- Yes OK.

 37

1 Good morning. I'm calling on behalf of Bell Inns and I'd be grateful if I could ask you a few questions about our restaurants.
2 Sure, go ahead./Do you know how often you have used the restaurants in the last six months?
3 Erm. Probably about three times./OK. And could you tell me what you think of the quality and friendliness of the staff?
4 Very good I think. No problems./That's fine. And finally, I was wondering if you had dinner alone or with colleagues or friends?
5 Actually it was with friends./Great. Thank you very much for your time.

Phone calls with customers/colleagues

22 Making appointments

 39

ERICH Hello this is Erich Binder again. Is that Cheng Ying?
CHENG Yes, hello Erich.
ERICH Sorry for interrupting you again Cheng, but it's about the time we arranged for the conference call.
CHENG Is there a problem?
ERICH Well, I'm calling to fix another time because Michael and Ana are busy this week. Do you mind if we postpone it to next week?
CHENG Let me check – one moment. I'm just looking at my diary. OK. Here we are. Which day are you thinking of?
ERICH Does Wednesday suit you?
CHENG No, not really. How about Thursday?
ERICH Morning or afternoon?
CHENG It doesn't matter to me. Which would be convenient for you?
ERICH We can make it after lunch – at two.
CHENG That sounds fine.
ERICH Thanks Cheng. So that's Thursday at two o'clock. I'll confirm it by email.
CHENG Talk to you all next Thursday. Bye.

 40

1 Hi Cheng. I'm calling about our meeting on Tuesday.
2 Oh yes?/I'm afraid Ana can't make it.
3 Oh dear. Never mind./Can we postpone it to Friday?
4 I'm afraid I'm unavailable on Friday./How about next Monday?
5 Morning or afternoon?/Would the morning suit you?
6 Sure. That sounds fine./Is ten thirty OK?
7 That's fine./Good. So that's next Monday at ten thirty.
8 Look forward to it. Bye./Thanks Cheng. Goodbye.

23 Inviting people

 41

- … so anyway the real reason I'm calling is because I'll be in Copenhagen next week on business. I'm staying at the Imperial Hotel so would you like to have a drink or something to eat in the centre?
- That would be great.
- How about meeting for dinner on Tuesday evening?
- Oh I'd love to but we're going out for a friend's birthday that evening. But why don't you join us at the restaurant?
- That's very kind of you but if you're going with someone else.
- It's a good friend. She won't mind. Especially as I only see you once a year.
- Well, I'd like that very much …

42

1 Hello?
2 Hi. It's Raymond./Hi Raymond. How are you?
3 Fine thanks. And you?/Very well.
4 Would you like to meet up for dinner tonight?/I'd love to but I'm going to the cinema with friends.
5 OK. How about going out tomorrow night?/That would be great.
6 OK. Good./But do you fancy coming to the cinema tonight?
7 I'd like that very much./Great. We're meeting at eight.
8 Which cinema?/It's the cinema on Geld street.
9 I know it. See you there./See you tonight. Bye.

24 Confirming arrangements

 43

ROGER Hi Melissa, it's Roger. I'm ringing to check everything's OK for Thursday.
MELISSA Yes, I think everything's done.
ROGER Have you booked the food?
MELISSA Yes, I booked the catering company a month ago. They're providing everything – tables, decorations, champagne, sandwiches – everything.
ROGER But what time are they arriving?
MELISSA I told them to come in the afternoon at three.
ROGER That's fine. Oh! Will they have finished by the time the guests start arriving?
MELISSA Well we don't open until six thirty, so that gives them plenty of time. I think they'll have left by about five.
ROGER Good.
MELISSA Roger – I do have one question about the press conference. Will the journalists be interviewing the artists at six thirty or later?
ROGER Probably between seven and seven thirty.
MELISSA So the artists need to be here at six forty-five at the latest.
ROGER Yes, I suppose so.
MELISSA Do they all know that?
ROGER I think so.
MELISSA I think I'll ring them – just to be certain.
ROGER Good idea. Thanks Melissa. I can see you've covered everything. I'll leave you to it.

 44

1 Hello Melissa. What time is my welcome to the Japanese journalists?/It's at ten forty-five.
2 Will I have finished my welcome to the French group by the time the Japanese arrive?/ Yes, you'll have finished half an hour before.
3 When is the French group interviewing the artists?/Between eleven and twelve.
4 What will the French group be doing while the Japanese are looking at the paintings?/They'll be interviewing the artists.
5 Will the French group leave the Buffet reception as soon as the Japanese arrive?/No, they won't. They'll be leaving fifteen minutes later.

25 A conference call

 45

PEMA Hello. Are you there Simon?
SIMON Hello?
PEMA Simon? Can you hear me?
SIMON Hi Pema. I can hear you. The line's a bit quiet.
PEMA Is that loud enough?
SIMON Yes. Fine.
PEMA OK. Thanks for joining us. I've also invited Mira today because she's in charge of staff at the new call centre in Bangalore.
MIRA Hello Simon.
SIMON Hello Mira. Is that right? Is that how I say your name?
MIRA Yes, that's right.
PEMA So Simon, have you had time to think about my email?
SIMON Yes I have.
PEMA And what do you think?
SIMON Well I understand your point about culture and that the language isn't so important and so I've been working on a course about British culture. So if the caller mentions something in the news for example, the person in India knows what they're referring to.
PEMA Let me just stop you for a second Simon because I know Mira wants to say something.
MIRA Hello Simon. I like the idea of a course in culture but I don't agree that it should only be culture. I think there are language problems – specially with idioms and slang and sometimes with accents.
SIMON Sorry, what was that? The line went quiet again.
MIRA I said problems with idioms, slang and accents.
SIMON Yes, I think you're right. The two things go together – language and culture. One idea I had for pronunciation was to do the training on the phone.
PEMA I like that idea.
SIMON We can listen to the people at the call centre and offer help.
PEMA I don't think that's the problem actually Simon. Is it Mira?
MIRA No. There's no problem with understanding our employees in Bangalore. It's the accents of the callers.
SIMON OK I see what you mean. So perhaps we can give them plenty of listening practice. OK. We can build that into the programme, no problem

PEMA Great.
PEMA So to summarize: Simon, you're going to send me your programme for the trainer coming to Bangalore and also a distance programme by phone. Is that right?
SIMON Yes – once Mira has sent me the results from her survey.
PEMA Yes, so Mira, you're going to speak to the teams.
MIRA Yes, and I think we need to record some of the calls and listen to the problems.
PEMA Yes, I agree. We need to find out a little more before deciding. OK. So let's speak again in two weeks – the same time?
SIMON/MIRA Fine.
PEMA I'll write up my notes from today and email them to you Simon. OK?
SIMON Great, thanks. Speak again in two weeks. Bye Mira.
MIRA Bye.
PEMA Bye Simon.

Commercial phone calls

27 Placing an order

 47

- Good morning. Spyline Products. Sales.
- Good morning. I've been looking at your catalogue and I'd like to place an order, please.
- OK. What would you like to order?
- Could I have two Voice Changers, please?
- Sorry, do you have the catalogue number for that?
- Sure. It's SL33VC.
- Thanks. That was two Voice Changers, wasn't it?
- That's right.
- OK. Anything else?
- I also need a Truth Teller at four hundred and seventy dollars.
- Was that one?
- Yes, just the one. And can I also order one Call Pass.
- OK. So that's two Voice Changers, one Truth Teller and one Call Pass.
- Oh and one more thing. I have a question about the Phone Protector, catalogue number SL36PP. Will it work with more than one phone at once or do you need one per phone?
- Err. I'm fairly certain you need one per phone.
- OK I'll order five of those, please.
- OK I'll write down five but I will check just in case you only need one. I'm sure you need more.
- Thanks. That's it I think. When can I expect delivery?
- We normally say two weeks.
- That's fine.
- What name shall I put on the invoice?
- It's Chandler. Chandler Security.
- Sorry, can you spell that?
- C-H-A-N-D-L-E-R Security.
- Thanks.
- Can I pay by credit card?

48

1. Good morning. Spyline Products. Sales./Hello, I'd like to place an order, please.
2. OK. What would you like to order?/Could I have two voice changers?
3. Sure. Do you have the catalogue number there?/Yes, it's S L double 3 V.
4. Thanks. What else would you like?/I also need a Truth Teller.
5. Sorry, what's the price?/Four hundred and seventy-eight dollars.
6. Thanks. Anything else?/Can I also order a Call Pass?
7. Sure. What's the catalogue number and price?/It's SL 35 CP at three hundred and five dollars.
8. Thanks. Anything else?/I'll order five Phone Protectors.
9. OK. Got that./When can I expect delivery?
10. In about two weeks./Can I pay by credit card?

28 Solving problems

49

- Good morning. Euro Deliveries.
- Hello, we asked your company to collect a package from us for delivery to Moscow.
- Do you have a reference number?
- Yes, it's YY-0788.
- One moment. Yes, one box of brochures for Moscow for Outsize Limited. The computer says we're going to collect it this afternoon. After two o'clock it says here.
- But the trade fair starts this afternoon. We ordered delivery for this morning.
- One moment ... the booking form says this afternoon.
- But it's going to be too late! We're meeting agents all day.
- OK. I'll send a courier straight away and I'll check flight times to Moscow.
- That would be great.
- And I'll call you back in about five minutes to let you know. OK?
- Thanks very much.

50

1. Good morning. Euro Deliveries.
2. Hello, we asked your company to collect a package from us for delivery to Moscow./Do you have a reference number?
3. Yes, it's YY-0788./OK. I'll send a courier straight away.
4. But isn't it too late for the flight to Moscow?/I'll check the flight times as well.
5. Thanks./And I'll call you back in five minutes to let you know. OK?
6. That would be great./Speak to you soon. Bye.

29 Complaining and handling complaints

51

- Hello. Moran Machinery. Karl speaking.
- Hello, I'm calling about a late order I placed two weeks ago.
- I see.
- It was a week late and then when we opened it yesterday there was only half the order.
- OK. I understand. Do you have a reference number for it?
- Erm. It was CP 66 SL.
- OK. Is that Mulgrave Industries?
- That's right.
- And so the order was a week late and you didn't receive all the items.
- No. And we can't use the items we have because they don't work without the other pieces of machinery.
- I'm sorry, but can I have the exact date of the order.
- Err yes. It was the fifth of June. And we need them today. We're already late with production on a job for someone else ...
- It was the fifth of June. OK. Let me see what I can do about this Mr ... ?
- Mr Sevin.
- And what's your contact number Mr Sevin?
- 0228 567 4673.
- OK. I'll call our warehouse Mr Sevin and then I'll call you right back. Is that OK?
- That's fine. Thanks very much.
- You're welcome.

52

- Hello. This is Mr Sevin. I'm afraid I'm unable to get to the phone right now. Leave a message after the tone.
- Hello Mr Sevin. This is Karl at Moran Machinery. I spoke to you a few days ago about a problem with a delivery. I'm really sorry for the mistake and I hope you've received the rest of the items. As I say, I do apologize and please ring me if you have any further problems. Goodbye.

53

1. Hello. Moran Machinery. Karl speaking.
2. Hello, I'm calling about a late order I placed two weeks ago./I see.
3. The order arrived a week late and then when we opened it yesterday there was only half the order./OK. I understand.
4. Well what are you going to do about it?/Do you have a reference number?
5. Erm. It was CP 66 SL./So it was a week late and you only received half the order.
6. That's right./I'm really sorry. Let me see what I can do about this.
7. OK./I'll call our warehouse Mr Sevin and then I'll call you right back. Is that OK?
8. That's fine. Thanks very much./You're welcome. Speak to you soon.

30 Selling on the phone 1

54

MARCO Good morning, my name's Marco Pani. I'm calling from Student Weekly.
MORADI Oh yes ...
MARCO Sorry, who am I speaking to?
MORADI I'm the human resources assistant manager.
MARCO Good morning Mr ... ?
MORADI Mr Moradi.
MARCO Good morning Mr Moradi. As I say I'm calling from Student Weekly and we're a newspaper which is only sold to students in universities and colleges ...

MARCO That's interesting. How many new graduates do you recruit a year?
MORADI It varies. Our division takes two or three trainee managers every year. But the company at national level employs between ten or twenty graduates per year. And then we have international placements ...
MARCO Great. I noticed you have a website. What percentage of applicants come from your website?
MORADI It's hard to say. We don't always find out exactly and we get a lot of enquiries via the Internet and our website from people who just aren't suitable.
MARCO So it sounds like you need more quality applicants ...
MORADI Yes, it's a problem.
MARCO What about newspaper advertising? How does that work for you?
MORADI It's OK. But again you receive applications from the wrong people ...
MARCO And advertising in national newspapers is so expensive ...
MORADI That's right ...

MARCO As I said, Student Weekly is sold directly in universities and we have a special feature for our readers next week on careers so your advert would appear on the same page.
MORADI I am interested, but I'll need to speak to someone first.
MARCO That's fine. Oh, before I forget, I don't think I mentioned that this offer also includes free promotion at a

careers fair in London in March. We always have a stand at it and represent our clients to over five thousand students …
MORADI OK. Well that might be useful, but as I say I just need to discuss it.
MARCO Right. Well can I send you a copy in the post so you can see the type of newspaper we are?
MORADI That would be useful.
MARCO Thank you for your time Mr Moradi. Would you mind if I called again later this week?
MORADI Erm. Well I'm away tomorrow …

31 Selling on the phone 2

 55

- Hello?
- Hello. Yes?
- Oh hello. I'm ringing about your advert in our local newspaper.
- Oh yes?
- It's the one for twenty per cent off if you buy before the end of the month.
- Oh OK. I know what you're talking about. Sorry, about that. I was just writing an email when you rang. Right. Yes. OK. Well perhaps I should take your name.
- It's McDonald.
- OK Ms McDonald. And you heard about us in the paper. Can I ask which one? Which paper?
- The Citizen.
- Today's Citizen?
- Actually it was yesterday's Citizen newspaper.
- Yesterday's. OK.
- I wonder if you could send me a brochure. To have a look at …
- … well how about I come and visit you?
- I think I'd rather have a look at the brochure first …
- It's really no problem. I'm visiting your area later this week anyhow so it's no trouble.
- Oh OK.
- So can I take your address?
- Erm. Thirty-six King's Street. Canterbury.
- And would Thursday be OK? At two?
- Erm. Yes I think so.
- Great. So I'll see you on Thursday at two Ms McDonald. It's been nice talking to you.
- Yes. Goodbye.
- Bye.

56

1 Good morning. Discount Wine. This is John speaking.
2 Oh hello. I'm ringing about your special offer on red wine this week. There's twenty per cent off on all wines./Can I just take down your name?
3 It's Mrs McDonald and I'm interested in a regular order of wines./I see.
4 I run a restaurant and we need a regular supplier./Can I ask how you heard about us?
5 A friend recommended your company to me./Would you like a brochure or can I visit?
6 I'd like a brochure first of all please./OK. Can I take your address?
7 Yes, it's the Wine Garden, thirty-six King's Street./Can I just read that back to you? It's the Wine Garden, thirty-six King's Street.
8 That's right./OK. I'll send you a brochure and then call you early next week.

Phrase bank

Essentials

Answer the phone	Good morning/afternoon/evening.
	Can I help you?
	Hello?
	Sales.
	… speaking.
	Hello. Three five one, two one one.
Offer help	How can I help you?
	How may I help you?
	What can I do for you today?
Ask to speak to someone	Can/Could I speak to …, please?
	I'd like to speak to …
	Is … there?
	Do you know when he's free?
Ask who's calling	Is that Diana?
	Can I have your name, please?
	(Can I ask) who's calling?
Say who's calling	It's … here.
	This is … (name) of … (name of company).
	I'm a friend/colleague of …
Greetings	Hello. How are you?
	Nice to hear from you again!
	I didn't recognize your voice!
	It's ages since we spoke.
Give a reason for calling	Can I speak to someone about …?
	I'm calling in connection with …
	The reason I'm phoning is …
	I'm phoning/calling to …
	It's with regard to …
	It's about …
Connect the caller	I'll put you through (to) …
	Let me just see if someone's available (to) …
	I'll try his number for you.
	I'll just connect you (to) …
	I'll transfer you (to) …

Ask the caller to wait	One moment. Do you want to hold? Can I just put you on hold? Please hold. Are you OK to wait a couple of minutes? Just bear with me a moment. Hang on a second.
Check the person who answers has time to talk	Is this a good moment? Have I rung you at a bad moment? Can we talk now or later? Do you have a second? Do you want me to call later? Are you busy right now?
Ask the caller to call back later	Do you mind calling back this afternoon? Sorry, can you call again later? Do you mind calling back this afternoon?
Explain the person is unavailable	Sorry, she's unavailable at the moment. She can't get to the phone right now. She's in a meeting/at lunch/out of the office. I'm sorry, but he's on another call.
Leave a message	Do you know how long he'll be? Do you know when she's free? Can I leave a message? Please ask him to call me back. Please say I called. Can you ask her to call me back? Can I leave my phone number?
Take a message	I don't know when she'll be back. Can I take a message? Can I give him a message? I'm just getting a pen. OK. Go ahead. What's it in connection with? Can you spell that? Anything else? Let me read that back to you. I'll give her your message.
Show you're listening/ show interest	I see./Right. /OK. I understand. That's fine/great. Is that right? Is that OK? Really?

Ask for repetition and clarification	Please speak up/more slowly. Can you repeat that? Would you mind saying that again? Do you mind repeating that? Speak more slowly, please. Sorry, I didn't catch that. I couldn't hear you, I'm afraid. I'm sorry; I don't speak English very well. Can you repeat that?
Clarify	Let me spell it. It's W-A-Y-N-E. Got that? Let me read it back to you. So that's 'A' as in 'Amsterdam'. It's thirty: three, zero.
End the call	Is there anything else I can help you with today? Sorry I'll have to stop you there. I'm expecting another call. I wonder if I could call you again in a month's time? Thank you for your time. It's been nice talking to you. Bye. Sorry but I must go now. Thanks for calling. Goodbye. Bye.
Refer to future contact	OK. See you at seven. Look forward to hearing from you. Bye. When can I expect to hear from you?

Everyday phone calls

Book a hotel/restaurant	I'd like to book/reserve a …
	How many … is that for?
	When/What time is that for exactly?
	Is that a …?
	Can I have a credit card number to secure the reservation?
	Can I take a contact number?
	Would you like confirmation in writing?
	Is there anything else I can do for you today?
	We look forward to seeing you …
Book transport	I'd like to book a …
	I need a …
	Are there any more … leaving today?
	Is there a …?
	How many … are there tomorrow?
	How much does it cost?
	What time is that for?
	How long does it take to …?
	Can it pick me up at a quarter past eleven?
Deal with problems	It's a bad/crossed/faulty line.
	My battery's very low.
	You're breaking up.
	The reception's terrible.
	I can't hear a thing.
	It's too noisy here.
	Hang up and try again.
	Let me call you back.
	Can you hear me OK?
	Can you speak up?
Leave a recorded message	Hello. This is …
	I'm afraid I'm out of the office/can't get to the phone right now.
	Please leave your message after the tone.
	Or call me on …
Leave a message on a voicemail/answer machine	Hello, this is … /my name's …
	Just calling to say …
	It's in connection with …
	Call me at the office.
	You can reach me at …
	I'll try calling again tomorrow.
	If you'd like to call me back/give me a ring, my number is …
	Look forward to speaking to you./Speak soon.

Inviting	Would you like to …?
	How about …?
	Why don't you join us …?
	Do you fancy …?
	That would be great.
	That's very kind of you …
	I'd like that very much.
	That sounds nice.
	Oh I'd love to (but) …
	Thanks very much (but) …
Make appointments	I'm calling to fix/arrange/make …
	Does Wednesday suit you?
	How about next Monday?
	Which would be convenient for you?
	Is ten thirty OK?
	Which day are you thinking of?
	Can we postpone it to Friday?
	I'm afraid I'm unavailable on … / I can't make it then.
	That sounds fine.
	So that's Thursday at two o'clock.
	I'll confirm it by email.
	Look forward to it. Bye
Manage a conference call	Are you there Simon?
	Can you hear me?
	Thanks for joining us today.
	The reason for this meeting is …
	… is in charge of …
	… wants to say something …
	So, to summarize …
	Let's speak again in …
Participate in a conference call	What do you think?
	How do you feel about …?
	I think that …
	In my opinion …
	I agree/disagree/don't agree.
	I like that idea.
	I see what you mean.
Place an order	I'd like to place an order, please.
	Could I have …
	Can I also order a …
	I'll order …
	When can I expect delivery?
	Can I pay by credit card?

Apologize/Solve problems	I'm really sorry. I'm afraid that … I do apologize. I'll send … I'll check … I'll call you back …
Complain	I'm calling to complain about … The items were late/don't work/are wrong … I'd like a …
Handle complaints	Let me see what I can do about this. Do you have a reference number for it? I see./I understand. I'll call our warehouse. So the order was a week late … I'm sorry, but …
Sell	I'm calling to tell you about/introduce … Would you be interested …? Can I ask how you heard of us? Did someone recommend us to you? The problem with …/Because of … We offer … I'll send you a brochure and then call you again early next week.

Answer key

1 Answering the phone

A

Person 1 (Main receptionist):
greets the caller
says her company's name

Person 2 (Sales receptionist)
says her department's name
offers help

Person 3 (Vitale Marini)
says his name
greets the caller

B

1 T 2 F 3 F 4 T

C

1 Good morning.
2 Hello.
3 Can I help you?
4 Can I speak to
5 speaking
6 It's

2 Making and taking calls

A

	Call 1	Call 2	Call 3
Does the person who answers know the caller?	N	Y	Y
Does the caller want to speak to the person who answers?	N	Y	N

B

The listening contains phrases 1, 2, 4, 6, 7, 9, 10, 11, 13, 14.

C

Answer the phone: 1, 3, 10
Offer help/Ask who's calling: 2, 5, 6, 13
Ask to speak to someone: 4, 8, 12, 14
Say who you are: 7, 9, 11

D

1 Can I help you?
2 This is Midori.
3 Can I speak to Walter?
4 Is Eric there?
5 It's Ann at AIC computing?

E

1 Is 2 Are 3 Do 4 Have 5 Can
1 d 2 e 3 a 4 c 5 b

F

1 Good morning. Can I help you?
2 Hello. Can you put me through to Vitale, please?
3 Certainly. Can I have you name, please.
4 Yes, it's Walter Geiger.
5 One moment Mr Geiger.
6 Hello. Vitale speaking.
7 Hi Vitale. It's Walter.
8 Oh hello Walter.
9 Do you have a second or do you want me to call later?
10 No, now is fine.

3 Reasons for calling

A

a) apply for a job
b) arrange a course
c) make a complaint
d) place an order
e) query an invoice
f) request a catalogue

B

Human Resources – apply for a job – call 4
After sales – make a complaint – call 3
Sales – place an order – call 6
Accounts – query an invoice – call 2
Training – arrange a course – call 5
Marketing – request a catalogue – call 1

C

1 to someone about   4 with regard to
2 in connection with   5 's about the
3 is because of   6 'd like to

D

1 ✓
2 ✓
3 (X) I'm calling to arrange a meeting.
4 (X) It's with regard to placing an order.
5 ✓
6 (X) I'm phoning to request a brochure.
7 (X) I'd like to speak to someone about the project.
8 ✓
9 ✓
10 ✓

E

1 put 2 deal 3 try 4 connect 5 transfer 6 back

4 Leaving messages

A

Message 1 – Call 1
Message 2 – Call 3
Message 3 – Call 2

B

1 b 2 b 3 c 4 b 5 b 6 a 7 a

C

1 b 2 d 3 g 4 c 5 f 6 a 7 e

D

1 tell   6 ask/tell
2 ask   7 ask
3 say   8 tell
4 tell
5 say

E

1 b 2 b 3 b 4 a

5 Taking messages

A

The mistakes are:
Name of caller: Martha Sterligova
Telephone number: 00 39 456 7110
www.m-sterligova.com/htm_test66.

B

1 b 2 d 3 e 4 g 5 a 6 i 7 c 8 j 9 f 10 h

C

1 Marogg
2 Palgimi
3 Hansen
4 Toimitusjohtaja
5 Lopo

F

Name of caller: Teixeira
Telephone number: 00 351 567 110
Urgent ✓
Message: Please email the report to teixlopo@lisboa-globe.pt

6 Asking the caller to wait

B

The caller speaks to three people.
1 b 2 a 3 e 4 d 5 f 6 c
The listening contains phrases 1, 5, 3, 4, 2.

C

1 or   4 moment/minute/second
2 couple   5 so
3 now   6 second/minute

D

1 'm putting
2 is ringing
3 'm looking
4 isn't answering
5 's working
6 'm just opening
7 're coming
8 'm just dealing
9 is running
The listening includes 1, 3, 4, 5, 8.

7 Asking for repetition and clarifying

A

1 S 2 D 3 S 4 D 5 D 6 S 7 D 8 S

B

1 understand + mind   6 mean + knows
2 speak + hear   7 got + read
3 say + catch   8 speak + repeat
4 's + speak   9 need + write
5 spell + be   10 hear + try

C

30th July
AF 335
3.50

D

The speaker uses techniques 1, 3, 4 and 5.

E

1 Engineer Eskola is arriving on the thirteenth of July.
2 So that's the end of July.
3 And he's coming from Tampere on flight A S three three five.
4 Not AS. AF. F as in Finland.
5 And did you say he leaves at three fifteen or lands at three fifteen?

8 Ending the call

A

1 c 2 c 3 b 4 c 5 b 6 a 7 a

B

1 Good   7 anything else
2 go   8 stop
3 See you   9 time
4 calling   10 nice/Bye
5 Look forward   11 When
6 much   12 again

C

Say goodbye: 1, 10
Give reason for ending: 2, 8
Refer to future contact: 3, 5, 11, 12
Thank the other person: 4, 6, 9
Offer help: 7

D

1 b   2 g   3 i   4 d   5 a   6 c   7 h   8 f   9 e

9 Language review 1

A

1 's calling   5 called
2 is   6 'll be
3 rung   7 're expecting
4 I'm calling   8 been

B

1 putting you through
2 call you back
3 hangs up
4 bear with
5 slow down
6 is running out
7 Hold on
8 speak up
9 pass on

C

1 have   5 call   8 talk
2 spell   6 ask   9 say
3 give   7 leave   10 tell
4 help

D

1 Give   3 answer   5 divert
2 take   4 respond   6 Make

E

say: A, H, take, wait
my: bye, I, time, Y
speak: E, me, P, read
you: do, Q, through, U

10 Booking hotels and restaurants

A

B

1 How may I help   5 Can I take (or) Can I have
2 How many   6 Can I take (or) Can I have
3 When is that for   7 Would you like
4 Is that a   8 Is there

C

1 13th   2 15th   3 1/5/78   4 09/08   5 25/12

D

1 I help you today?   5 people is that for?
2 that for?   6 smoking or non-smoking?
3 have your name, please?   7 exactly?
4 spell that?   8 anything else?

E

Sunday (2)
Monday (2)
Tuesday (2)
Wednesday (2)
Thursday (2)
Friday (2)
Saturday (3)
January (4)
February (4)
April (2)
July (2)
August (2)
September (3)
October (3)
November (3)
December (3)
March, May and June are missing.

11 Booking transport

A

The woman books a sleeper ticket on a train and a cab.

1 some
2 any
3 an
4 many
5 a
6 much

B

1 i 2 b 3 e 4 c 5 d 6 g 7 f 8 h 9 a

C

The speakers say: ten minutes past one, thirteen thirty-three, a quarter past eleven

D

1 ✓
2 It leaves **at** thirteen forty-five.
3 Can you pick me up **in** half an hour.
4 ✓
5 ✓
6 I normally go on holiday **in** the summer.
7 ✓
8 ✓
9 ✓
10 He arrives **on** the thirty-first.

12 Dealing with telephone problems

A

Problem on the line: 1, 5
Problem using a mobile: 2, 4
Problem with dialling: 3

B

1 bad
2 noisy
3 wrong
4 low
5 dead

C

1 really
2 absolutely
3 very
4 too
5 too
6 so
7 such

D

	1	2	3	4	5
Speak up	✓	✓			
Call back straight away				✓	
Call back later	✓	✓			
Hang up	✓				
Try a different number				✓	✓

E

1 Sorry, can you speak up?
2 Let's put the phone down.
3 Try calling again later.
4 Let me call you back in five minutes.
5 Try him on extension 376.
6 How about sending me it by email?
7 Hang up and ring the other number.

13 Recorded information and phone menus

A

a) leave a message? 6
b) wait? 5
c) hang up? 3
d) press a number? 2
e) call back? 4
f) call a different number? 1

B

1 options
2 replace the handset
3 'm unable to/at the present moment
4 delay
5 the following
6 currently busy

C

Message 1: 5
Message 2: 1
Message 3: 2
Message 4: 6
Message 5: 4
Message 6: 3

D

1 Press
2 Dial
3 Try
4 speak
5 Pick
6 Put
7 switch
8 Select
9 hold

E

Thank you for calling our cinema customer hotline. /
Please select one of the following options: /
for details of our films, / press 1; / to book tickets. / press 2. /

14 Leaving voicemail messages

A

Reason for calling: to discuss a few ideas after meeting at conference
Contact details: contact on 00417586178 between 9-12

B

1 Introduce yourself: a, g
2 How you know the person: e
3 Give reason for calling: h, i
4 Give contact details: c, f
5 Give availability: b
6 Give alternative: j
7 End message: d

C

1 Hello, Bernard. My name's Stephan Bougin. I work for Hankel SA in Bern. (a)
2 You might remember that we met at a conference in February in Lyon. (g)
3 You suggested I call you at some stage to discuss a few ideas. (e)
4 Sorry I didn't call sooner but it's been busy since I got back. (d)
5 Anyway, it's just to let you know I'm interested. (h)
6 You can contact me on 00 41 758 6178. That's 00 41 758 6178. (f)
7 I won't be in this afternoon but you can normally reach me between nine and twelve. (i)
8 Or I'll try calling you again tomorrow. (b)
9 Look forward to speaking to you. Goodbye. (c)

15 Language review 2

A

1 any
2 a
3 information
4 much
5 a little
6 many
7 are
8 some

B

1 with
2 up
3 up
4 on
5 off
6 out
7 back

C

1 It's **just** to let you know I'll be back at three.
2 It's **just** a quick call to confirm our meeting.
3 Can you email me **just** in case?
4 I'm **just** calling to say …
5 Could you **just** give me his number?
6 I'm afraid I'm rather busy **just** now.
7 You only **just** caught me. I was about to leave.
8 I was speaking to him **just** last week.
9 I'll be with you in **just** a second.
10 Please **just** leave me your number.
11 I **just** wanted to check the prices in your brochure.
12 **Just** a single please.

D

1 spend
2 Take
3 Make
4 having
5 Take
6 pass on
7 Do

E

1 4 2 3 3 5 4 5 5 4 6 4 7 4 8 6 9 6 10 4

16 Sounding friendly and polite

A

A smile makes your voice sound friendly and polite and makes you and your colleagues feel better.

B

1 = ☺ 2 = ☺ 3 = ☹ 4 = ☺ 5 = ☹
6 = ☹ 7 = ☺ 8 = ☹ 9 = ☺ 10 = ☹

D

1 name
2 to speak to
3 she's in a meeting.
4 talking to someone.
5 you / to
6 what
7 a pen

E

1 Sorry, could I have your name, please?
2 One moment please Mr Chiu … I'm sorry, she isn't in the office today.
3 I'm afraid he's talking to someone.
4 Would you like to hold?
5 Would you like me to take a message?
6 Sorry, one moment. I'm just looking for a pen. OK. Go ahead.

17 Planning a call

A

1 f 2 b 3 a 4 c 5 g 6 d 7 e

18 Telephone manner

A

1 b 2 c 3 a

B

1 interpersonal skills
2 out-going
3 communication
4 friendly and polite
5 sympathetic
6 ability to persuade
7 ability to listen
Sally is the Customer Care Telephonist.

C

1 a 2 a 3 b 4 a 5 b 6 a 7 a 8 b 9 a

D

1 c 2 d 3 f 4 a 5 e 6 b 7 g

19 Small talk

A

In some countries such as the UK, phone calls often start and end with small talk. It is an important part of building business relationships. In other countries such as Sweden or German small talk is not as important on the phone.
Make small talk. 3
Introduce the reason for calling. 4
Greet the other person. 1
Make small talk. 6
End the call. 7
Ask how the other person is. 2
End the reason for calling. 5

B

Hi Diana. It's Midori. 1
How old are the kids now? 3, 6
Actually, the reason I'm calling is… 4
Anyway I must go. 7
Sorry, I didn't recognize your voice! How are you? 2
Do you fancy coming to stay? 3, 6
It's in connection with… 4
We might take a holiday next year. 3, 6
We really must speak again soon. Bye 7

C

1 Really
2 Great.
3 That's a pity
4 Me too
5 wonderful
6 I'll tell him
7 Yes

20 Formal and informal

A

1 c 2 h 3 e 4 a 5 j 6 g 7 f 8 b 9 d 10 i

B

1 Kozma
2 It's/an advert
3 I'm/Bell Inns
4 a message
5 him/I called
6 nice to hear from you
7 to
8 give me/next week
9 So when/you again
10 sorry/she's
11 sorry
12 call
13 see/you then
14 I must
15 your time
16 speak/soon/bye

C

1 would be prepared
2 you have used
3 what the reason was
4 what you think
5 if you could choose
6 how you rate

21 Language review 3

A

1 a 2 h 3 j 4 b 5 e 6 f 7 c 8 g 9 d 10 i

B

1 can't
2 must
3 have to
4 should
5 could
6 would
7 will

C

1 long
2 are
3 about
4 much
5 many
6 was
7 far
8 often
9 may

D

1 about
2 for
3 for
4 in
5 to
6 about

E

1 What time does the flight land?
2 Could I borrow your mobile?
3 Is Yukiko there, please?
4 Would you try his number?
5 When will she be back?

F

2 Please speak after the tone.
3 Is that right?
4 Please call me back on three five one, two five nine.
5 It's three five, six one, four five two.

22 Making appointments

A

1 No.
2 Because Michael and Ana are busy this week.
3 Later.
4 His diary.
5 Wednesday.
6 Thursday at two o'clock.
7 By email.

B

1 b 2 d 3 f 4 e 5 i 6 a 7 g 8 c 9 h 10 j

1 fix
2 are busy
3 postpone it
4 are you thinking of
5 suit you
6 How about
7 convenient
8 can make it
9 fine
10 So that's

C

1 convenient
2 Tuesday doesn't
3 our interview back
4 about (we say) three
5 in mind
6 make it on the first
7 anytime next month
8 Thursday at two

D
1 It's me
2 fixing
3 make
4 OK
5 busy
6 put it back

23 Inviting people

A

The man and woman both invite each other.
1 to have
2 to come
3 meeting
4 join
5 playing

The conversation includes phrases 1, 3 and 4.

C
1 That
2 I'd like
3 I'd
4 That's very kind

D
1 to
2 in
3 on
4 at
3 I'm afraid I'm not **in** the office at the moment.
4 ✓
5 Let's meet **on** the second floor. Take the lift.
6 ✓
7 ✓
8 ✓
9 Why don't you meet me later on for a drink **in** the hotel bar?
10 I normally get home by six in the evening.

24 Confirming arrangements

A
1 3
2 6.30
3 7.30

B
1 T 2 F 3 T 4 F 5 F

C
1 Have/booked
2 booked
3 are/arriving
4 open
5 'll have left
6 Will/be interviewing
7 'll ring

Past simple 2
Present perfect 1
Present simple 4
Present continuous 3
Future simple 7
Future continuous 6
Future perfect 5

D
1 'm phoning
2 will have finished
3 hasn't called
4 'll be
5 close
6 're holding
7 Have/reserved
8 will/have arrived
9 are looking
10 won't be

25 A conference call

A
1 Staff at the new call centre in Bangalore.
2 British culture.
3 She disagrees and thinks there should be culture and language.
4 Listening (to accents).
5 Write up her notes and email them to Simon.

B
1 c 2 e 3 g 4 a 5 h 6 f 7 o 8 b 9 m 10 k
11 i 12 l 13 j 14 n 15 d

C
1 there
2 hear
3 joining
4 reason
5 mean
6 think
7 idea
8 What
9 speak
10 agree

26 Language review 4

A
1 joining
2 to call
3 to play
4 playing
5 to arrange
6 meeting
7 coming
8 to have
9 to go
10 seeing

B
1 I'll put you through.
2 Can I call you back?
3 Hang up the phone and try again.
4 Let me read that back to you.
5 I'm afraid he's tied up at the moment.
6 Please pass this message on. / Please pass on this message.
7 Just bear with me a second.
8 Let me take your name down. Let me take down your name.
9 Try looking up his number in the phone book.
10 Can you speak up?

C
1. at (5pm)
2. on (989 546)
3. at (www.macmillanenglish.com)
4. (2) to (4)
5. in (Sardinia)
6. for (3)
7. on (the ground)
8. to (an Italian)
9. in (the morning)
10. at (a nightclub)/on (Christmas Eve)

D
1. Hello, this is Marco speaking.
2. Does Tuesday suit you?
3. I'm really interested in the job.
4. I'm sorry but he's out of the office today./I'm afraid he's out of the office today.
5. I'm really sorry about this.
6. Can you tell him I called?/Can you say I called?
7. Sorry but I must go now./Sorry but I have to go now.
8. I'll call you back tomorrow.
9. I agree with you.
10. She's calling in connection with an invoice.

E
1. Are you <u>there</u>?
2. Can you <u>hear</u> me?
3. <u>Thanks</u> for <u>joining</u> us today.
4. The <u>reason</u> for this <u>meeting</u> is …
5. <u>What</u> do you <u>think</u>?
6. I <u>see</u> what you <u>mean</u>.
7. I <u>like</u> that <u>idea</u>.
8. Let's <u>speak</u> again <u>soon</u>.

27 Placing an order

A
1. Call Pass
2. Phone protector
3. Truth teller
4. Voice changer

B
1. SL33VC 3. $470 5. SL36PP
2. 2 4. 1 6. 5

C
1. catalogue
2. place an order
3. Could I have
4. also need
5. can I also order
6. thing
7. a question
8. I'll order
9. delivery
10. credit card

28 Solving problems

A
Reference number: YY-0788
Collection time: After 2pm
Contents of package: brochures
Destination: Moscow

B
1 c 2 e 3 a 4 b 5 d

C
For making predictions: It's going to be too late!
For timetables or programmed events: The trade fair starts this afternoon.
For arranged events (eg meetings): We're meeting agents all day.
For promising action: We're going to collect it this afternoon.
For a planned future event (or intention): I'll call you back in five minutes.

1. 'm meeting
2. leaves
3. 'll contact
4. 's going to be
5. 'll cancel
6. is going to be
7. 'm leaving
8. 'll call
9. 'm going to work
10. 's going to work

D
Promise 1: To send a courier straight away
Promise 2: To check flight times

E
1 c 2 f 3 a 4 b 5 e 6 d

29 Complaining and handling complaints

A
The order was late and incomplete.
We opened it yesterday and there was only half the order.
We need them today.

B
1. was
2. broke
3. bought
4. paid
5. get
6. made
7. cost
8. have
9. gave
10. sent

C
1 c 2 g 3 b 4 e 5 f 6 a 7 d

D
1. 'm afraid
2. really sorry
3. do apologize

30 Selling on the phone 1

A

The speakers mention newspaper adverts, the Internet and careers fairs.
1 Human resources.
2 In universities and colleges.
3 Between ten and twenty a year.
4 No. Many aren't suitable.
5 Advertising is expensive.
6 Promotion at a careers fair.
7 A copy of Student Weekly.
8 Call again later in the week.

B

Stage 1: d, g
Stage 2: b, i
Stage 3: a, e
Stage 4: c, f
Stage 5: h, j

D

1 What are you
2 What does your
3 How many people do you
4 Why do you

E

1 c   2 a   3 d   4 b

F

1 Thank you for your time.
2 Would you mind if I call again next week?
3 I look forward to speaking to you again.

31 Selling on the phone 2

A

The sales rep doesn't follow rules a, b and c.

B

1 e   2 c   3 d   4 f   5 a
6 g   7 b   8 f   9 e   10 g

D

1 b   2 f   3 a   4 e   5 g   6 d   7 c

E

2 a brochure
3 Paul Powers
4 the budget
5 products
6 Marek
7 the supplier

32 Language review 5

A

1 calls   6 heard
2 opened   7 'll check
3 I've just received   8 was
4 's just talking   9 called
5 will have finished   10 going to have

B

1 Where   6 Are
2 How many   7 Who
3 What   8 When
4 Does   9 Do
5 Which   10 Would

1 j   2 a   3 b   4 f   5 i   6 d   7 c   8 e   9 g   10 h

C

1 products
2 payment
3 connection
4 delay
5 attachment
6 flight
7 manufacturer
8 information

D

2 With so
3 Due to
4 As
5 As a result
6 Therefore
7 In response
8 hence

E

1 I'm <u>really</u> sorry for that.
2 I <u>do</u> apologize.
3 I'm afraid I <u>just</u> don't know.
4 Monday will be <u>too</u> late.
5 I'm <u>so</u> grateful for your help.
6 I'd <u>love</u> to join you.
7 That sounds <u>great</u>!
8 We're <u>not</u> very happy with our supplier.
9 I'm sure your products are all <u>excellent</u>.
10 I can bring one over <u>personally</u>.